Southam

An A–Z

Terry Paine played in 801 League and Cup games for Saints, scoring 183 goals.

Dean Hayes

S.B. Publications

DEDICATION

To Saints' fans everywhere. . .

First published in 1998 by S. B. Publications,
c/o 19 Grove Road, Seaford, East Sussex BN25 1TP

ISBN 1 85770 170 4

Designed and typeset by CGB Lewes
Printed by MFP Design and Print
Longford Trading Estate, Thomas Street,
Stretford, Manchester M32 0JT

Southampton Football Club A–Z

A

ABANDONED MATCHES

AN abandoned match is one which is called off by the referee when it is in progress, because conditions do not permit it to be completed.

During the club's great FA Cup run of 1925, the Saints were leading Exeter City 5–0 in the first round with just ten minutes left to play when the fog descended and the referee was forced to abandon the game. Some Southampton fans went on to the pitch to remonstrate with the referee, but he would not change his decision. Fortunately, the Saints won the replay 3–1 and went all the way to the semi-final before losing 2–0 to Sheffield United.

ABERDEEN TOURNAMENT

ALL the games in this competition at the start of the 1981–82 season were played at Pittodrie. In their opening match, goals from George, Holmes and Keegan gave the Saints a 3–1 win over Manchester United, but then despite a Steve Moran goal, the host club won a rather one-sided final against Southampton 5–1.

ADAMS, BILL

ALTHOUGH half-back Bill Adams joined Southampton from Guildford midway through the 1925–26 season and made his debut in the opening game of the 1927–28 campaign, he had to wait until 1930–31 before becoming an established member of the Saints' first team.

The following season he was made club captain and was the only ever-present in the Southampton side. He continued to be a mainstay of the Saints' first team, also playing a number of games at full-back, but in

1936, after appearing in 205 League and Cup matches, he joined West Ham United.

He made his Hammers' debut at The Dell and scored one of the goals in a 2–0 win for the visitors, a feat he had only achieved three times in his stay at Southampton. He did not stop long at Upton Park and moved to Southend United, where he ended his league career.

AGGREGATE SCORE

SOUTHAMPTON'S highest aggregate score in a domestic competition is 8–0, which they achieved in two Football League Cup matches – Wrexham (home 5–0 and away 3–0) in 1979–80 and Rochdale (away 5–0 and home 3–0) in 1990–91.

In the European Cup Winners' Cup of 1976–77, the Saints beat Carrick Rangers 5–2 away from home, then 4–1 at The Dell to win 9–3 on aggregate.

ALLEN, TOMMY

Tommy Allen joined Southampton from Sunderland on a free transfer in May 1920 and in 1920–21, the club's first season in the Football League, his goalkeeping was a major factor in the Saints' consistency.

In 1921–22, Allen was an ever-present as the Saints won the Third Division (South) Championship and kept twenty six clean sheets in forty two games – still a club record. He went on to play in 323 League and Cup games, notching up a record 291 League appearances for a Southampton goalkeeper before leaving The Dell in the close season of 1928 to play for Coventry.

He later had spells with Accrington Stanley and Northampton before retiring from the game.

ANDREWS, LEN

SIGNED from Reading, Len Andrews was a goalscoring left-winger who could also take penalties. He made his debut for the Saints in a 2–2 home draw against Northampton Town on the opening day of the 1912–13 season, by the end of which, he scored nine out of nine penalties. On 10 April 1915 he scored his only hat-trick for the club in a 4–2 home win over Brighton and Hove Albion. He played for the Saints during the First World War but in July 1919 he left The Dell to rejoin Reading. Two seasons later he was back on the south coast and in 1921–22 played his part in helping the Saints win the Third Division (South) Championship.

During 1924, after he had scored thirty five goals in 164 first team games, he left The Dell for a second time to play for Watford.

ANGLO–ITALIAN CUP

AFTER Swindon Town won the Football League Cup in 1969 they were ineligible to qualify for the Fairs Cup, as they were then a non-First Division side. Instead, they organised a match against the Italian League Cup winners, AS Roma, and played for the Anglo-Italian League Cup.

The following year was born the Anglo-Italian Cup for club sides from the two countries who had no involvement in Europe and each country provided six entrants between 1970 and 1973. It was discontinued in 1974 but returned in 1975 as a two-legged match between the winners of the FA Cup and the Italian Cup. In 1976, the Saints played Napoli but lost 4–1 on aggregate.

APPEARANCES

TERRY PAINE holds the record for the number of League and Cup appearances in a Southampton shirt with a total of 809 games to his credit between 1956 and 1974.

The players with the highest number of appearances are:

	League	FA Cup	Lg Cup	Europe	Total
Terry Paine	709(4)	51	37	8	805(9)
Mick Channon	507(3)	40(2)	28	16	591(5)
Nick Holmes	437(7)	45	38	12	532(7)
Tommy Traynor	433	34	13	0	480
Albert Shelley	392	38	0	0	430
Eric Day	398	24	0	0	422
John Sydenham	341(2)	31	21	4	397(2)
Matthew Le Tissier	321(36)	29(1)	36(6)	0	386(43
Sid Woodhouse	351	15	0	0	366
Hugh Fisher	297(5)	22(2)	17(1)	8(1)	344(9)

ARMSTRONG, DAVID

DURHAM-born midfield player David Armstrong began his career with Middlesbrough and in nine seasons at Ayresome Park played in 359 league games, including at one stage going seven seasons without missing a single game. In the summer of 1981 he joined Southampton for a record fee of £600,000 and made his debut in a 4–1 home win over Wolverhampton Wanderers. He quickly fitted into the Saints' midfield and scored fifteen goals, an impressive total in the face of some ultra-defensive football.

Although naturally a left-sided player, his reading of the game allowed him to play in a variety of positions. He was an obvious choice as the club's captain as he had already represented England against Australia during his days with Middlesbrough. His talents earned him further caps against West Germany and Wales while at The Dell.

He had played in 262 League and Cup games for the club when contractural disputes led to him leaving The Dell and joining Bournemouth, where he ended his league career. He joined Waterlooville FC as general manager in March 1995 having previously spent a number of years as an officer for Football in the Community, latterly at Reading.

ARNOLD, JOHNNY

LEFT-WINGER Johnny Arnold signed from Oxford City and made his Southampton debut in a 3–0 home win over Millwall in April 1929. He was, at this time, qualifying as a professional cricketer for Hampshire but the following season underlined his potential as a goal scoring winger by netting seven times in the eighteen games in which he played. During the

1931–32 season he was the Saints' top scorer with twenty league goals, including netting in five consecutive games towards the end of the season. Midway through the following season, he had scored eleven goals in twenty six games, including a hat-trick in a 4–3 home win over West Ham United when, along with Mike Keeping, he joined Fulham.

Within a month of his arrival at Craven Cottage, he had been capped by England in their match against Scotland. He played for Fulham until the outbreak of the Second World War but he continued to open the batting for Hampshire until 1950, scoring 21,596 runs at an average of 32.92. He appeared in one Test match for England, thus becoming one of the few men to have represented his country at both sports. After his retirement from active sport, he became a first class umpire, a position he held for twenty years.

ATTENDANCES – AVERAGE

THE average home league attendances for Southampton over the last ten seasons have been:

1987–88	14,543	1992–93	15,382
1988–89	15,590	1993–94	14,754
1989–90	16,463	1994–95	14,685
1990–91	15,413	1995–96	14,820
1991–92	14,070	1996–97	15,099

ATTENDANCES – HIGHEST

THE record attendance at The Dell is 31,044 for the First Division match with Manchester United on 8 October 1969. The Reds won 3–0 with goals from Best, Burns and Kidd.

ATTENDANCES – LOWEST

THE lowest attendance at The Dell for a first class fixture is 1,875 for the Second Division game against Port Vale on 30 March 1936 which the Saints lost 1–0.

AWAY MATCHES

SOUTHAMPTON'S best away win came on 22 January 1977 when they won 6–0 at Carlisle United. The club have also scored six goals away from home in the league on three other occasions, winning 6–1 at Mansfield Town in the 1958–59 season, 6–2 at Chelsea in 1967–68 and 6–2 at Wolverhampton Wanderers in 1976–77. The Saints also scored six goals in a 6–1 first round FA Cup win at Walton and Hersham in the 1957–58 season.

Southampton's worst defeat away from home is the 8–0 scoreline inflicted on the club by Tottenham Hotspur (1935–36) and Everton (1971–72). The Saints also conceded eight goals in a league match on 10 November 1951 when they lost 8–2 at Bury.

AWAY SEASONS

THE club's highest number of away wins came in 1921–22 when they won nine of their twenty one matches when winning the Third Division (South) Championship.

In 1933–34, the Saints failed to win one single away game but still managed to finish fourteenth in the Second Division.

B

BAKER, GRAHAM

LOCAL-born midfield player, Graham Baker, made his Southampton debut in a televised Second Division match against Blackpool at The Dell and made a dream start, scoring inside the first minute of a game the Saints went on to win 2–0.

He was a versatile hard-working player, appearing in nine different positions for the club before establishing himself in the Number 11 shirt, when he was rather surprisingly sold to Manchester City in 1982.

Although he suffered two serious injuries during his spell at Maine Road, he did help City win promotion to the First Division in 1984–85. In the summer of 1987, after appearing in 134 games for the north-west club, he returned to The Dell for a second time. After a loan spell at Aldershot he moved to Craven Cottage where he ended his league career with Fulham, having scored thirty six goals in 195 League and Cup games for the Saints.

BALL, ALAN

Football mad as a boy, Alan Ball went for trials with both Wolves and Bolton but was rejected by both. In the end, it was only the persistence of his footballing father, Alan Ball senior, that persuaded Blackpool to sign him after Ball junior had gone to Bloomfield Road for a trial.

After making his debut for the Seasiders against Liverpool at Anfield at the age of seventeen, he established himself as a first team regular. He quickly gained international honours and in August 1966 joined Everton immediately after his scintillating contribution to England's World Cup victory.

In his early days at Goodison Park, Ball combined constant midfield creativity with a strike rate that many a forward would have been proud of, netting fifty six times in three seasons. With Howard Kendall and Colin Harvey, he was part of the celebrated midfield which swept Everton to the League Championship in 1969–70.

In December 1971, Ball joined Arsenal for £220,000, a new British record fee. In his first season at Highbury, he helped guide the club to the FA Cup Final against Leeds but after five years with the London club, he was transferred to Southampton for £60,000.

Alan Ball.

He made his debut for the Saints in a 1–1 draw at Plymouth Argyle and though he arrived too late that season to make any impact in the promotion race, he made a distinctive contribution to the club returning to the top flight in 1977–78.

He played in every match during the Saints' first season back in Division One, his never-say-die attitude influencing the much younger Southampton players, especially Steve Williams. While at The Dell, Ball spent the summer months playing for Vancouver Whitecaps in the NASL but at the end of the 1979–80 season he decided to try his hand at management and returned to Bloomfield Road.

It was not a happy experience and when in March 1981, Lawrie McMenemy offered him the chance to return to The Dell, he accepted. In 1981–82 Ball had a magnificent season, helping the club finish seventh in the First Division after they had led the table for much of the campaign. Midway through the 1982–83 season he decided to try his luck in Hong Kong. He returned to England to play for Bristol Rovers.

When he finally hung up his boots, Ball joined Portsmouth for the 1983–84 season and in 1987 took them into the First Division. He later managed Stoke City and Exeter City before taking charge at

Southampton. With Lawrie McMenemy working behind the scenes, it was a new look set up which Saints fans had dreamed of for months and starting with two wins, Ball managed to keep the club in the Premier League.

In 1994–95, in his first full season at the helm at The Dell, the club finished in tenth place, but midway through the close season he left to take charge at Manchester City. Resigning from Maine Road at the start of the 1996–97 season, Ball returned to League management last season with former club, Portsmouth.

BATES, TED

TED BATES came from a sporting family. His grandfather, Willie, played cricket for Yorkshire and England and also represented his country at rugby and his father, Billy, also played cricket for Yorkshire and Glamorgan as well as football for Leeds United and Bolton Wanderers.

Bates joined Norwich City straight from school but when his manager Tom Parker moved to Southampton, he was one of the players he took with him to The Dell. He soon forced his way into the first team and made his debut in a goal-less draw at Swansea Town in December 1937. Despite the war interrupting his career, he still managed to turn out for the Saints while serving in the Army and when he was demobbed he returned to League action with Southampton.

Good in the air, he formed a deadly partnership with Charlie Wayman to terrorise the Second Division's defences. Though not as prolific a scorer as Wayman, Bates scored sixty four goals in 212 League and Cup games, including a hat-trick in a 4–2 home win over Bury in March 1952. He also appeared in 183 wartime games, scoring sixty goals and in his playing career with the Saints he turned out in every position for the club, including goalkeeper, when he once took over when Hugh Kelly was injured.

In October 1952, Bates was appointed coach and assistant trainer. He did well as reserve team coach and seemed the logical choice to succeed George Roughton as manager in September 1955. When he took control, the club had a £60,000 overdraft but within five years not had he only sorted out the finances but in 1959–60 he led the club to promotion to the Second Division.

It was Ted Bates' greatest discovery, Terry Paine who headed the goal which brought First Division football to The Dell in 1966.

The Saints found it difficult to hold on to their First Division status and it took all Bates' guile and knowledge and some wheeling and dealing on the transfer market to consolidate the club's position. Amongst his many signings were big Ron Davies from Norwich City for a club record fee of £55,000, and a youthful Mick Channon. His judgement was very sound, for over the next few seasons Davies, aided by Terry Paine, scored plenty of goals to ensure that the club did not return to the Second Division. In fact, the Saints established themselves as one of the country's leading clubs and in 1969 qualified for Europe for the first time.

When Ted Bates retired in December 1973 to become a director of the club he was the longest-serving manager in the Football League.

BEASANT, DAVE

DISCOVERED by Wimbledon while playing for non-League Edgware Town, Dave became a regular for the 'Dons' and did not miss a league match from the beginning of 1981–82 until he left for Newcastle United in the summer of 1988 – a total of 304 consecutive Football League matches.

During that time he won both Division Four and Division Two Championship medals as the club moved to Division One. His last game for the Dons was the sensational 1988 FA Cup Final against Liverpool in which he saved John Aldridge's penalty – the first spot kick saved in Cup Final history – and Wimbledon held on to take the trophy back to South London.

At St James' Park he had little opportunity to further his reputation and after just six months on Tyneside he returned to London to play for Chelsea. He helped the Stamford Bridge club win the Second Division

Championship and in the summer of 1990 won international recognition when he came on as substitute goalkeeper for England against Italy. After a disastrous match against Norwich City in September 1992, Ian Porterfield, the then Chelsea boss, told him he would never play for the club again. He had loan spells at Grimsby Town and Wolverhampton Wanderers before joining Southampton for £300,000 in November 1993.

Nicknamed 'Lurch', he made his debut for the Saints in a 1–0 defeat at Everton on 4 December 1993 and played in the remaining twenty five league games of that season. Sharing the goalkeeping duties with Bruce Grobbelaar the following season, he kept the Zimbabwean international on the bench for all but two games in 1995–96 and put together an impressive thirteen clean sheets.

He has now appeared in more than 100 League and Cup games for the Saints and has produced a number of outstanding performances in the last few seasons to help the club in their fight against relegation.

BENALI, FRANCIS

AN England Schoolboy international, he made his Football League debut as a substitute at home to Derby County in October 1988.

After a further couple of appearances as a substitute, he got a chance to impress following a long-term injury to Micky Adams.

Benali was originally a left-winger but he was given an extended run at left-back and has since shown that he can play in the centre of defence and in midfield. He is a strong, competitive player, who is aggressive in the tackle, but his poor disciplinary record has often cost him his place in the side. Although an excellent striker of the ball, he is still looking for his first goal after almost 300 games in Southampton colours.

BEST STARTS

SOUTHAMPTON were unbeaten for the first seven games of the 1950–51 season when they won four and drew three of the opening matches before losing 1–0 at Blackburn Rovers on 11 September 1950. Unfortunately, the Saints could not maintain this standard and ended the season in twelfth place in the Second Division.

BIGGEST DEFEATS

The club's biggest defeats in the Football League occurred on 28 March 1936 and 20 November 1971 when they lost 8–0 to Tottenham Hotspur and Everton respectively. They also conceded eight goals on 10 November 1951 when they lost 8–2 at Bury. The Saints' biggest defeat in the FA Cup is 5–0 by Manchester City in a second round tie on 5 February 1910. The club's biggest defeat in the Football League Cup was 7–1 by Watford on 2 September 1980.

Southampton's worst home defeat in the Football League is 6–0, a scoreline inflicted upon the club by both Plymouth Argyle on 5 December 1931 and Brentford on 9 March 1959.

BIGGEST WINS

THE club's biggest win in the Football League is the 8–0 victory over Northampton Town in a Third Division (South) match on 24 December 1921. The Saints also scored eight goals in a league match on 3 November 1928 when they defeated Blackpool 8–2.

The Saints' biggest win in the FA Cup was the 7–1 defeat of Ipswich Town in a third round tie on 7 January 1961. The 5–0 victories over Derby County on 8 October 1974; over Wrexham on 28 August 1979; and over Rochdale on 25 September 1990 is the club's best scoreline in the Football League Cup.

The club's best win in the league away from home is the 6–0 win at Carlisle United on 22 January 1977.

BLAKE, JOE

BEFORE signing for Southampton in 1905 Joe Blake had previously played for Ilford, Tottenham and Cowes. He was, at the time, an amateur and worked in the shipbuilding industry at Cowes. Despite making a goal scoring debut for the Saints in a 5–1 home win over Millwall on 6 October 1906, he had to wait until the 1909–10 season before establishing himself in the first team. He remained at The Dell until 1915 when he took up full-time employment at Thorneycrofts as a draughtsman. During the First World War, he turned out for both Southampton and

Thorneycrofts, scoring five goals in forty six appearances for the Saints.

Southampton held his registration and so when the game resumed in 1919–20, he played for the Saints before leaving towards the end of the season to play for Thorneycrofts again.

BLYTH, MEL

MEL BLYTH began his football career with non-League Great Yarmouth before joinig Scunthorpe United in November 1967. He had only made twenty seven league appearances for the Irons when he moved to Crystal Palace. He played in 216 league games for the Selhurst Park club before signing for Southampton for a fee of £60,000 in August 1974.

He played his first match for the club in a 2–0 defeat at Bristol City on 21 September 1974 and went on to appear in all of the thirty four remaining league games that season. In fact his impact was such that he was voted the supporters Player of the Year. In 1975–76, he played an important part in the Saints' FA Cup victory and had a particularly outstanding game in the final against Manchester United. He returned to Selhurst Park on loan in November 1977 before signing for Millwall the following year after having played in 122 League and Cup games for Southampton.

BOND, KEVIN

KEVIN BOND began his league career with Norwich City during the 1975–76 season when his father, John, was the Carrow Road club's manager. He scored memorably at both ends in successive games in March 1980 and was Norwich City's Player of the Year. He won two England B caps with the Canaries but in September 1981, after a spell with Seattle Sounders, he followed his father to Manchester City.

In the autumn of 1984, Lawrie McMenemy signed Bond for a fee of £70,000, as a replacement for Reuben Agboola. He was appointed captain in 1986-87 and went on to play in 170 League and Cup games before signing for Bournemouth in the summer of 1988.

After having played in more than 100 league games for each of his four clubs, he accepted a one year contract under Alan Ball at Exeter City, after which he hung up his boots.

BOYER, PHIL

AFTER being released by Brian Clough at Derby County, Phil Boyer signed for York City, where he found himself playing alongside Ted

MacDougall. He scored twenty seven goals in 109 league games for York before joining Bournemouth. His form for the Dean Court club, where he netted forty six goals in 141 league outings led to Norwich City buying him for £145,000, a club record fee at the time.

At Carrow Road, he was capped by England and with MacDougall alongside him, the Canaries enjoyed two exciting seasons. He had scored thirty four goals in 116 league games when, in August 1977, he joined Southampton to fill the gap left by the recently departed Mick Channon.

His intelligent forward play paid immediate dividends when he made his Saints' debut in a 1–1 home draw against Brighton and Hove Albion on the opening day of the 1977–78 season. He was the club's leading goal getter as they finished runners up in Division Two.

In 1979–80 Boyer was again the Saints' top scorer with twenty three league goals, including three hat-tricks, against Derby County (home 4–0), Crystal Palace (home 4–1) and Bristol City (home 5–2).

The arrival of Kevin Keegan meant that Boyer had to move on and in November 1980 he joined Manchester City, where sadly an injury curtailed his career. He went to play in Hong Kong before returning to England to become player/manager at Grantham Town. He later scouted for Graham Carr at Northampton, Blackpool and Maidstone United.

BRADFORD, ARTHUR

ONE of the club's earliest utility players, Arthur Bradford appeared in six different positions including a game in goal. He was signed from a Walsall works team and played his first game for the Saints in a goal-less draw at Crystal Palace in April 1924.

Bradford was another of Southampton's unsung players, going on to appear in 319 League and Cup games in thirteen seasons with the club. He played his last game in a 1–0 home defeat by Port Vale in March 1936 when he left to become the licensee of a pub.

Although he only scored six goals in his time at The Dell, his all-round abilities were sorely missed. He continued to play non-League football after ending his days with the Saints, turning out for Cowes on the Isle of Wight.

BROTHERS

THREE brothers – Danny, Rodney and Ray Wallace – played for Southampton on 22 October 1988 in the match against Sheffield Wednesday at The Dell, which the Owls won 2–1. It was the first time in sixty eight years that three brothers had played in the same First Division side.

Arthur Turner, who was born in Farnborough, became the first Hampshire-born player to represent his country when he played for England against Ireland at Dublin in March 1900. In only his eighth Southern League game for the Saints, he scored four goals in a 9–0 win over Chatham, eventually ending with twenty four goals in seventy eight Southern League appearances. His younger brother, Harry, also graduated through the same South Farnborough team but not possessing as much skill as Arthur, only appeared in fifteen Southern League games for the Saints before leaving The Dell.

BROWN, EDDIE

ONE-TIME theological student Eddie Brown, who had studied in the Channel Islands before being evacuated during the war, was one of the game's fastest strikers. He started his career with Preston North End, where he scored fourteen goals in thirty one league games, and moved to Southampton in September 1950 in a part exchange deal which saw Charlie Wayman go in the opposite direction.

Brown, one of the game's great characters, made his Southampton debut in a 2–0 home win over Leeds United and ended that 1950–51 season as the club's top scorer with twenty goals in thirty six appearances.

He started the next year's campaign in similar vein and had scored twelve goals in twenty one games, including a hat-trick in a 5–2 home win over Nottingham Forest, when he decided he could not settle at The Dell and asked for a transfer.

He moved to Coventry City and continued to score on a regular basis, netting fifty goals in eighty five league games. He later played for Birmingham City and Leyton Orient, taking his total of goals scored to 190 in 399 league appearances for his five clubs.

BURNSIDE, DAVID

BRISTOL-born David Burnside's first Football League club was West Bromwich Albion which he joined as an outstanding schoolboy footballer. His ability at juggling a football became famous when, as a youngster, he displayed these talents to crowds at The Hawthorns just before kick off. Later in 1960, he won a competition organised by the *Sunday Despatch* to discover the British player who could produce the most consecutive headers. Burnside, with 495, was way ahead of Tommy Harmer of Tottenham Hotspur on 286. He had played in 127 league games for Albion and represented England at Youth and Under–23 level when he signed for Southampton in October 1962.

After making his debut in a 1–1 draw at Leeds United, he soon settled into the side and ended the season with eighteen goals in thirty nine League and Cup appearances, including four goals in the club's fine FA Cup run. Unfortunateley, there were occasions when he found it difficult to put his undoubted skills to good use and in December 1964, after scoring twenty six goals in seventy League and Cup games, he joined Crystal Palace for a fee of £12,000.

After appearing in fifty six league games for the Selhurst Park club he later played for Wolverhampton Wanderers, Plymouth Argyle, Bristol City and Colchester United before being appointed manager of Bath City in 1972. He also played for Minehead and Bridgewater Town before becoming involved in running FA coaching courses.

C

CAMPBELL, ALEC

WHEN at King Edward's School, where he excelled at both football and cricket, he played for England at amateur level in an international against Holland, the only known occasion on which a schoolboy has represented his country at that level.

He was only fifteen when he made his Southampton debut against Millwall in the Southern League, but his performances in his early games soon alerted the bigger clubs and in the summer of 1909, he left The Dell to join Glossop. He later had a short spell with West Ham United before returning to play for the Saints in 1914.

At the outbreak of war he joined up, but still managed to play some football for the Saints, appearing in fifty six wartime matches. When normal football resumed after the hostilities, Campbell was made club captain and led the Saints to the Third Division (South) Championship in 1921–22. He left The Dell in 1926 to play for Poole Town, so ending an eighteen year association with the club.

CANN, SYD

A FORMER England Schoolboy international, Syd Cann began his footballing career with the club in his home town, Torquay United, before leaving to join Manchester City, where he played in the 1933 FA Cup Final side against Everton. In 1935 he signed for Charlton Athletic but on the outbreak of the Second World War he joined the Army Physical Training Corps and he reached the rank of warrant officer.

At Charlton he met Bill Dodgin and after the war he became his assistant at The Dell, combining the duties of trainer and masseur. In the summer of 1949, when Dodgin moved to Fulham, Cann was promoted to the vacant manager's job. In his first season in charge at The Dell, the Saints missed promotion on goal average with fifty two points and a goal average of 1.333 against Sheffield Wednesday's 1.395.

However, in December 1951 he resigned after disagreements with the board, although he stayed on as secretary for a short time. He later took Sutton United to two FA Amateur Cup Finals before becoming manager of Wycombe Wanderers.

CAPACITY

THE total capacity of The Dell in 1997–98 was 15,000.

CAPS

THE most capped player in the club's history is Peter Shilton who won forty nine caps for England.

CAPS (ENGLAND)

THE first Southampton player to be capped by England was Jack Robinson when he played against Wales in 1899. The most capped player is Peter Shilton with forty nine caps.

CAPS (NORTHERN IRELAND)

THE first Southampton player to be capped by Northern Ireland was Dick Rowley when he played against Wales in 1929. The most capped player is Chris Nicholl with thirty seven caps.

CAPS (REPUBLIC OF IRELAND)

THE first Southampton player to be capped by the Republic of Ireland was Jimmy Dunne when he played against Switzerland in 1937. The most capped player is Tony Byrne with fourteen caps.

CAPS (SCOTLAND)

THE first Southampton player to be capped by Scotland was Jack Robertson when he played against England in 1899. The second was Ian Black, who played against England in 1948.They are the only two Southampton players to have been capped by Scotland, each making just one appearance .

CAPS (WALES)

THE first Southampton player to be capped by Wales was Bert Hodgkinson when he played against Ireland in 1908. The most capped players are Ron Davies and Barry Horne who both won twenty three caps each.

CAPTAINS

CHARLES BROMLEY was the Saints' first captain.He moved to London to study dentistry and continued to make special journeys to Southampton for cup matches. He was replaced by George Carter, a fine full-back who captained the club for eight years. Jack Farrell was the Saints' captain when they first won the Southern League title in 1896–97 and again the following season. Harry Wood replaced him as captain in 1898–99 and in his first season led the club to their third consecutive Southern League Championship. Wood captained the club for seven seasons but on his departure to Portsmouth, the Saints made the astonishing announcement that the captain would be named before each game.

When Southampton entered the Football League in 1920–21, their captain was Alec Campbell and the following season he led them to the Third Division (South) Championship. He remained captain for six years before being replaced by Arthur Dominy.

A number of players then captained the club before Cliff Huxford, a solid, dependable wing-half, led the Saints to the Third Division Championship in 1959–60.

When Southampton won the FA Cup in 1976, it was Welsh international full-back Peter Rodrigues who climbed the steps to the Royal Box to receive the trophy from the Queen.

On the subject of captaincy, the club created a record on 7 March 1981 when they played Manchester United, fielding a side that contained four men who had captained England – Channon, Watson, Ball and Keegan, with the latter scoring Saints' goal in a 1–0 win.

CASE, JIMMY

JIMMY CASE was an amateur with South Liverpool before going to Anfield in May 1973. In the next eight years he made well over 200 League and Cup appearances, scoring forty five goals. He had a ferocious shot that produced a number of spectacular goals including the equaliser

against Manchester United in the 1977 FA Cup Final. In his stay at Anfield, he won three European Cup medals, four League Championship medals, a UEFA Cup winners' medal and a few runners-up medals as well.

During the summer of 1981 he signed for Brighton in a £350,000 transfer deal and helped them to a Wembley Cup Final.

He joined Southampton towards the end of the 1984–85 season as a replacement for Steve Williams and soon showed that he had lost none of his tenacity. He made his Saints' debut in a disastrous 5–1 defeat at Tottenham Hotspur and went on to play in 264 League and Cup games for the club until he joined Bournemouth in the summer of 1991. He later had spells for Halifax and Wrexham before being appointed manager of Brighton and Hove Albion in November 1995.

CENTURIES

THERE are eight instances of individual players who have scored 100 or more League goals for Southampton.

Mick Channon is the greatest goalscorer with 185 strikes during his two spells with the club. Other centurions are Terry Paine with 160; Bill Rawlings 156, George O'Brien 154, Eric Day 145, Derek Reeves 145, Matthew Le Tissier 140 and Ron Davies with 134.

Mick Channon and Terry Paine hold the club record for the most consecutive League appearances – 160. Other players to have made more than 100 consecutive appearances during their careers are Eric Day, 154; Bert Shelley, 141; Eric Webber, 134; Phil Boyer, 122; Terry Paine, 110; Hugh Fisher, 107; Terry Paine, 103; and Charlie Sillett, 102.

CHADWICK, ARTHUR

HE began his footballing career with his local side, Church, after which he moved to Accrington and then Burton Swifts before signing for Southampton in 1897.

Chadwick arrived at The Dell as a right-half but soon successfully converted to centre-half. He gained two England caps in that position and played in the Saints' 1900 FA Cup Final defeat against Bury. He was a fine penalty-taker but was allowed to leave the club in May 1901 to join Portsmouth. Three years later he played for Northampton Town and, after a short spell with Accrington, he became player/manager of Exeter City in 1908.

He guided the Grecians through their Southern League period and was in charge when they joined the Football League in 1920. He left Exeter to manage Reading in January 1923 but resigned when the Southampton position became vacant and in October 1925 became the Saints' new team manager.

After only one season he took the Saints to the semi-finals of the FA Cup but he had to sell the club's best players so Southampton could survive. Shrewdly, though, Chadwick bought new players and at the end of the 1928–29 season the club finished fourth in the Second Division, their best position in the Football League at that time. Two fairly uneventful seasons followed and in May 1931 he decided to leave the game.

Sadly, Arthur Chadwick died five years later, while watching a match at Exeter City.

CHADWICK, EDGAR

IN the 1890s Edgar Chadwick was one of the great names of football. His first senior club was Blackburn Olympic and he had one season with with Blackburn Rovers before joining Everton in the summer of 1888.

An inside-left of great talent, his left-wing partnership with Alf Milward was probably the best in the league. He won seven England caps, scoring after just thirty seconds on his debut against Scotland in 1892.

With Everton he won a League Championship medal and two FA Cup runners-up medals but after scoring 110 goals in 300 League and Cup games he left to play for Burnley. A year later he decided to move to Southampton in the Southern League and made his debut at Luton Town where he scored a goal in the Saints' 4–3 win. He ended the season as the club's top scorer with fourteen goals and played a major role in the Saints' winning the League Championship. In 1901–02 he helped the club reach the FA Cup Final but then bought out his contract with Burnley, who still held his registration as a league player, and joined Liverpool. Although not as prolific a scorer as in his Everton days, he had netted twenty two goals in sixty one League and Cup games.

He was reputed to be the first Englishman to coach abroad, when in 1908, he worked with teams in Holland and Germany. Eventually he tired of football and returned to Blackburn to pursue his trade as a baker.

CHAMPIONSHIPS

SOUTHAMPTON have won a divisional championship on two occasions. The first was in 1921–22, only the club's second season in the Football League, when Saints embarked on an unbeaten run of nineteen games from 5 September 1921 to 14 January 1922. This included two runs of five consecutive victories and an 8–0 win over Northampton Town, still the club's record victory in the Football League.

As the season drew to a close, it became a two-horse race between the Saints and Plymouth Argyle for the Championship and the one promotion spot. The Home Park club beat the Saints 1–0 and then played out a goalless draw at The Dell to surge ahead in the race for the title. The Saints clawed themselves back into contention with 1–0 wins at Newport County and Merthyr Tydfil – results which left the club's level on points with just one game to play. Southampton duly beat Newport County 5–0 and with Plymouth surprisingly losing to Queen's Park Rangers, the Third Division (South) Championship came to The Dell.

The Saints second Championship success came in 1959–60 when they scored 106 goals in winning the Third Division title. The club were able to field a settled side and midway through the season were four points ahead of their nearest rivals and with two games in hand seemed certain of promotion. Yet many of their fans could remember those days of the 1940s when promotion seemed equally as certain. However, this time the club maintained the consistency that had been lacking before, and with Derek Reeves scoring a record thirty nine league goals for them, the Saints finished two points ahead of Norwich City.

CHANNON, MICK

ONE of the greatest forwards ever to play for Southampton – and he has scored more goals for the club than any other Saints' player.

He was spotted by Bill Ellerington when playing in his native Wiltshire and although Bert Head, the Swindon Town manager, wanted to sign him, Channon's father, a keen Southampton supporter persuaded his son to join the team from The Dell.

He was two months short of his sixteenth birthday when he played and scored for the Saints' reserve side as the club's youngest ever reserve player. He made his first team debut at home to Bristol City on 11 April 1966, scoring the Saints second goal in a 2–2 draw.

In 1966–67, Southampton's first season in the top flight, he only made one league outing but the following season, after Ted Bates had decided to sell Martin Chivers, he was given a long run in the side. In 1969–70 he was the club's top scorer and won the first of nine England Under–23 caps when he played against Sweden.

Channon was Southampton's leading goalscorer for the next six seasons with a best of twenty one in 1973–74. The following season he netted twenty league goals including hat-tricks against Oxford United (away 4–0) and Bristol Rovers (home 3–0). He also scored four Cup goals including another hat-trick in a 5–0 League Cup third round tie win over Derby County.

In 1975–76, he again netted twenty league goals, hitting a hat-trick in a 4–0 home win over Portsmouth. This was the season that Southampton won the FA Cup, beating Manchester United 1–0 in the final. Channon was a key member of the Saints' side and scored a hat-trick in a 4–0 fifth round replay win over West Bromwich Albion. Channon's last hat-trick for the club came the following season when he netted all three goals in Southampton's 3–3 draw at home to Blackpool. His goal scoring feats brought him full international recognition and in 1972 he won the first of forty six England caps when he played against Yugoslavia.

Sensing he had achieved all he could as a Southampton player, he asked for a transfer and in the summer of 1977 he joined Manchester City. After two fairly disappointing seasons at Maine Road, Lawrie McMenemy brought him back to The Dell and in the 1982 close season, Channon parted company with the club for a second time, having scored 215 goals in 580 League and Cup games.

He then had brief spells with Newcastle United and Bristol Rovers before joining Norwich City. He gave the Canaries three excellent years service and helped them to win the Milk Cup in 1985. He was thirty seven when Norwich released him and he signed for Portsmouth to play under his old Southampton colleague Alan Ball. He scored six goals in forty games for the Fratton Park club before seeing out his career with Finn Harps.

He is now a racehorse trainer but Southampton fans who were privileged to see Mick Channon play can fondly remember each goal being celebrated with his unique windmilling-arm salute.

CHIVERS, MARTIN

HAVING played for Southampton and Hampshire at youth level and for Southampton's nursery side, CPC Sports, Martin Chivers signed professional forms for the Saints in August 1962 and made his debut in a 1–0 home win over Charlton Athletic the following month. In 1963–64, he finished the season as the club's joint leading league goalscorer. His twenty one goals came from only twenty eight games and included a hat-trick in a 5–1 home win over Swindon Town. That season also saw him win the first of twelve England Under–23 caps while at The Dell, when he played against France.

In the Saints' promotion-winning season

of 1965–66, Chivers scored thirty goals in his first twenty nine outings including four goals in a 9–3 home win over Wolverhampton Wanderers and a hat-trick as Cardiff City were beaten 5–3 at Ninian Park. Although he failed to score in his last ten games that season, he had played a huge part in the club reaching Division One for the first time.

Chivers was a big, strong forward and had a splendid tutor in the centre-forward's art, playing alongside Welsh international Ron Davies. In 1966–67 the couple scored more than fifty league goals but Chivers became restless at The Dell and in the autumn of 1967, the Southampton board agreed to his transfer request.

In January 1968, Spurs paid a record fee of £125,000 to sign the big man, with Frank Saul, valued at £45,000, moving to The Dell as part of the deal. Chivers, who had scored 107 goals in 189 League and Cup games, soon became the first Southampton-born man to play in England's forward line. Much of his time at White Hart Lane was plagued by a series of injuries but he still found time to score 174 goals in 367 League and Cup outings and win twenty four full England caps.

He left Spurs for £80,000 to join the Swiss club, Servette, and on his return to England played for Norwich City and Brighton and Hove Albion, but 'Big Chiv' was no longer up to the demands of league football. He tried his hand at management with Vard of Norway, Dorchester Town and Barnet before retiring from football due to injury in December 1982.

CLARKE, COLIN

SOUTHAMPTON was the sixth club of this much-travelled striker. Colin Clarke's family moved from Newry to Ipswich when he was twelve and so consequently he joined the Portman Road club as an apprentice. He failed to make the grade with Ipswich and joined Peterborough United on a free transfer. After playing in eighty two league games for the London Road club he joined Tranmere Rovers after a loan spell at Gillingham. At Prenton Park he scored twenty nine goals in the 1984–85 season, in which Birkenhead side just missed out on promotion to the Third Division.

In the summer of 1985 he signed for Third Division Bournemouth, where his goal scoring feats won him the first of thirty eight international caps for Northern Ireland and the attention of a number of top foreign clubs, including Torino of Italy. His performances for Northern Ireland in the 1986 World Cup convinced Saints' boss, Chris Nicholl, that Clarke had the ability to succeed in the top flight and in June of that year he paid £400,000 for his services.

Clarke made immediate history by becoming the first Southampton player to score a hat-trick on his debut in a 5–1 win over Queen's Park Rangers on the opening day of the 1986–87 season. He followed this up with another three goals in a 4–1 home win over Newcastle United in October 1986 and ended the season as the club's top scorer with twenty league goals. He then suffered from injuries and had a loan spell back at Bournemouth before joining Queen's Park Rangers. One season later he signed for Portsmouth for a club record fee of £415,000 and scored twenty seven goals in 107 first team appearances before retiring from the game.

CLAWLEY, GEORGE

IN an era when the position received scant, if any, protection George Clawley was one of the most reliable goalkeepers He began his career with Crewe Alexandra before joining Stoke in August 1894. However, his appearances for the Potters were limited, due to the presence of Bill Rowley, and in 1896 he was one of a number of players who left Stoke to play for Southampton St Mary's in the Southern League.

He was an ever-present for two seasons in which the club won and retained the Southern League Championship, and captain for the 1897–98 season. After two seasons on the south coast, during which time he played for Hampshire and the Southern League, he returned to Stoke for a year before going back to the Southern League, this time with Tottenham Hotspur. He made his debut for the White Hart Lane club in September 1899 but broke his leg the following month. Out of the side until April 1900, he had not played enough games to qualify for a Southern League Championship medal, but more than compensated for that the following season when he played in all Spurs' matches in their victorious FA Cup run.

He was splendid at dealing with corners and crosses and played in an international trial match in 1903, yet major representative honours eluded him. He returned to The Dell in 1903 and was Saints' regular 'keeper in their Southern League Championship side the following year and remained with the club until 1907 when he became landlord of the Wareham Arms Hotel in Southampton.

CLEAN SHEET

THIS is the colloquial expression to describe a goalkeeper's performance when he does not concede a goal. Tommy Allen in 1921–22 had twenty six clean sheets from forty two matches as the Saints won the Third Division (South) Championship.

COCA COLA CUP

see Football League Cup

COCKERILL, GLEN

HAVING played non-League football for Louth Town, Glen Cockerill signed for Lincoln City and made his Football League debut in an eventful 5–4 win at home to Northampton Town in February 1977. After some good performances he was transferred to Swindon Town but when Lincoln decided they wanted him back eighteen months later, in a drive for promotion to the Second Division, they had to part with nearly £30,000 more than they sold him for in the first place. In his two spells with the Sincil Bank club he played in 213 League and Cup games, scoring thirty six goals.

In March 1984 he joined Sheffield United, helping the Blades secure promotion to the Second Division but in October 1985, Chris Nicholl made Cockerill his first signing when he was appointed manager of Southampton. He soon settled into the Saints' side and played a significant part in the club reaching the FA Cup semi-final in 1986. After that, he missed very few matches and formed a strong midfield partnership with Jimmy Case and Barry Horne. He went on to appear in 346 League and Cup games for Southampton before leaving The Dell in December 1993 to join Leyton Orient on a free transfer.

He proved to be an inspirational captain for the Brisbane Road club, appearing in ninety seven first team games before being released at the end of the 1995–96 season.

COLOURS

FOR their first match the Saints wore white tunics with a diagonal red sash, but for the 1890–91 season specially manufactured shirts of cherry and white squares were worn. The club's colours changed again five seasons later when it was agreed that the Saints' tops would be red and white halves. In 1896–97 there was yet another change to red and white striped shirts and blue shorts. It was to be the last change for eighty years, although in 1934-35 the Saints switched to wearing striped stockings in an effort to help players find each other more easily.

On 27 January 1951, Southampton played at Sunderland in a fourth round FA Cup tie, wearing a kit of amber jerseys and black shorts borrowed from the Hampshire Regiment. Sunderland used a set of black and white striped shirts loaned by Newcastle United. The colour change benefited the Roker Park club, which won 2–0.

On 15 November 1958, the Saints beat Woking 4–1 in the first round of the FA Cup and wore unusual crimson and blue quartered shirts, the colours of the Hampshire County FA XI.

The club's present colours are red and white striped shirts, black shorts and red and white hooped stockings. The Saints' change colours are white shirts, white shorts and blue stockings.

CONSECUTIVE HOME GAMES

DURING the 1900–01 Southern League season, the club played two extraordinary intense sequences of five home games in succession. The first sequence was played in twenty eight days, from 6 October to 3 November, and saw the Saints win all five matches beating Bristol Rovers 5–3; Reading 1–0; Kettering Town 4–3; Gravesend 6–0; and Millwall 2–1. The second sequence was played in thirty five days, from 8 December to 12 January, and again Southampton won all five games, beating Watford 1–0; Luton Town 5–0; Tottenham Hotspur 3–1; West Ham United 3–2; and New Brompton 5–0.

The club also played five consecutive home games in the 1903–04 season, winning four and drawing one – New Brompton 4–0; Swindon Town 2–0; Fulham 2–0; Queen's Park Rangers 2–1; and Reading 1–1. In both these seasons the Saints won the Southern League title.

CRICKETERS

THERE have been eleven Southampton players who have been cricketers of real note.

Victor Barton, who replaced Ralph Ruffell in goal for the Hampshire Senior Cup semi-final match against Portsmouth in February 1893, scored 6,204 runs for Hampshire at an average of 25.01. Charles Robson, who served Hampshire as a batsman and wicket-keeper and captained the county for four years was appointed Saints' captain in 1895. Herbert Ward who scored six goals in nine Southern League appearances for the Saints, supposedly died from sunstroke while playing for Hampshire in a county cricket match, although a later verdict diagnosed typhoid fever.

Charles Burgess Fry, who played sixteen games for Southampton, was one of England's best cricketers for many years. For Sussex he scored 20,656 runs at 56.82 and for Hampshire 3,829 at 58.90. At international level he represented England in twenty six Tests, scoring 1,223 runs at 32.18 and a highest score of 144 against Australia at the Oval in 1905. Fry had many other talents and equalled the world long jump record, stood as a Liberal candidate for Parliament three times, represented India at the League of Nations and declined the throne of Albania.

Philip Mead's only appearance for Southampton was as goalkeeper in a goal-less draw at home to West Ham United in December 1907, although he played in a number of reserve games as a forward. He scored more runs for Hampshire than any other player – 48,892 at 48.84 and for England, scored 1,185 at 49.37, with a best of 182 against Australia at the Oval in 1921.

Alec Campbell, who captained Southampton to their first divisional championship in 1921–22, also played for Hampshire. Arthur Holt who scored forty six goals in 206 league games for the Saints, scored 2,853 runs at 22.46 for Hampshire, later becoming their coach. Johnny Arnold, who scored a record twenty one goals for Southampton from the left-wing in 1931–32, scored 21,596 runs for Hampshire at 32.92, with a top score of 227 v Glamorgan in 1932.

Don Roper, who scored forty goals in 120 league games for Southampton before making his name with Arsenal, played a couple of games for Hampshire and Henry Horton, a tough tackling wing-half, played cricket for both Worcestershire and Hampshire, scoring 21,536 runs at 33.49 for the latter named county. Laurie Fishlock, an England amateur international, scored 22,138 runs for Surrey and appeared in four Tests for England.

CROWD TROUBLE

ON 26 November 1898, the Saints were leading Millwall 4–1 in a Southern League match at the Den when the referee mistakenly ended the game ten minutes early. Realising his mistake, he tried to bring the teams back, but the home crowd had invaded the pitch and refused to disperse. Millwall were fined £5, which was later rescinded on appeal, and the match was completed five months later at the Dell before a Western League game.

CURTIS, ALAN

ALAN CURTIS began his league career with Swansea Town and took part in the Vetch Field club's steady climb from the Fourth Division to the First, winning fourteen Welsh caps on the way. He had scored seventy two goals in 248 league games for the Swans when he was transferred to Leeds United. Sadly for him the deal did not work out and after just twenty eight league appearances for the Yorkshire club he rejoined Swansea.

In November 1983, Lawrie McMenemy spent £80,000 in bringing the Welsh international to the Dell and although he continued to win caps for his country, he never really produced his early

Swansea form for the Saints. He made his Southampton debut in a 3–1 home win over Stoke City but failed to hold down a regular first team spot and in March 1986 he was loaned to Stoke City. At the end of the 1985–86 season, after he had scored seven goals in sixty five League and Cup games, he returned to Wales to play for Cardiff City. Three years later he returned to the Vetch Field for a third spell with Swansea before hanging up his boots.

CURTIS, GEORGE

INSIDE-FORWARD George Curtis began his league career with Arsenal, playing in two games in the 1938–39 season. His debut was a home fixture against Blackpool on 10 April 1939.

During the Second World War he served in India as a corporal in the Royal Air Force. After the resumption of league football in 1946–47, he played in eleven league games before being transferred to Southampton for £8,000, in part exchange for Don Roper.

Curtis was tall and willowy and made ball control look easy. After making his Saints debut in a 1–1 draw at Doncaster Rovers on the opening day of the 1947–48 season, he went on to become an important member of the early post-war Southampton sides. He stayed five seasons at the Dell, appearing in 183 League and Cup games. Curtis then played for French club Valenciannes in 1952–53 before returning to England as player/coach at Chelmsford City. By this time, he had become a qualified coach and over the next twenty years held positions at a number of clubs as well as coach to the England Youth team, the Sudan and the Norwegian national teams.

D

DAVIES, RON

HOLYWELL-BORN Ron Davies began his football career at Chester, where he was made to hurdle wearing army boots during training, an experience the Welsh international later claimed gave him extra power when jumping for crosses. He had scored forty four goals in ninety four games for Chester when in October 1962 he joined Luton Town. At Kenilworth Road he netted twenty one goals in thirty two games including four against Norwich City, his next club. Davies arrived at Carrow Road in September 1963 for £35,000, a record fee for both clubs. At Norwich, he scored fifty eight goals in 113 league games, including twenty six in one season, and when he was sold to Southampton for £55,000 in August 1966 there was an outcry in East Anglia.

Ron Davies.

Davies, already capped by Wales, made his Southampton debut in a 1–1 draw against Manchester City on the opening day of the 1966–67 season. In his first season in the top flight he scored thirty seven goals in forty one league games, including four in a 6–2 win over Aston Villa and hat-tricks against Leicester City (home 4–4), and Burnley (home 4–0). This was a remarkable record in a Southampton side that struggled all season against relegation. In the course of netting those thirty seven goals he scored in ten successive league games for the club.

In 1967–68 he scored twenty eight goals to make him the First Division's joint top scorer for the second year in succession, including four in a 6–2 win at Chelsea. He top scored again the following season with twenty goals in thirty eight games and in 273 League and Cup games for the club, he scored 149 goals.

He was signed by Portsmouth in the summer of 1973 and appeared in all the club's competitive matches the following season, scoring sixteen goals. The season after that he signed for Manchester United but unfortunately for their supporters his powers were waning and he registered only eight substitute appearances without scoring. After a short spell at Millwall he moved to California to coach. He now lives in Florida, where he coaches Orlando Lions.

DAY, ERIC

DURING the Second World War Eric Day was a commando and in 1945–46 played in two wartime games for the Saints, scoring a goal in a 3–2 home win over Tottenham Hotspur. When league football resumed he had to wait until 16 November 1946 before making his first team debut in a 3–1 defeat at Millwall.

Day was a fast and aggressive forward who was able to play on either flank, and defenders did not relish playing against him. In 1947–48 he was the club's second joint top scorer with ten goals, including all three in the 3–0 home win over Chesterfield. In 1950–51 he netted twelve league goals in thirty seven games to finish second in the Saints' scoring charts to Eddie Brown. The following season, in which he was ever-present, he again reached double figures as he did in 1952–53 when he scored his second hat-trick for the club in a 6–1 home win over Blackburn Rovers.

After the Saints were relegated to the Third Division (South), Day was moved into a more central position and responded with twenty six goals in forty six league games in 1953–54. The following season he went one better, netting twenty seven goals in forty four league outings before producing his best season, in terms of goals scored, in 1955–56. Then this ever reliable forward again topped the scoring charts with twenty eight goals, including a hat-trick in the 3–1 home win over Crystal Palace.

During his eleven seasons at The Dell, Eric Day was a model of consistency, scoring 156 goals in 422 League and Cup games before leaving to play non-League football for his home town club, Dartford.

DEBUTS

MIDWAY through the 1905–06 season, the Saints paid Belfast Distillery £300 for the signature of their Irish international centre-half, Sid Johnston. After only twelve minutes of his debut in a Western League game at Tottenham Hotspur, he was injured and never kicked another ball for the club. The Saints' directors sent him to London for an operation but the big Irishman refused to have anaesthetic and returned to Belfast. Tommy Mulgrew joined the Saints from Newcastle United for £7,000 in the summer of 1954 and scored after just fifteen seconds when making his debut in a 6–4 home win over Brentford.

Northern Ireland international centre-forward Colin Clarke is the only Southampton player to score a hat-trick on his debut for the club, which he did in a 5–1 win over Queen's Park Rangers on the opening day of the 1986–87 season.

DEFEATS – FEWEST

DURING the 1921–22 season, Southampton went through the full forty two match programme and only suffered four defeats, all away from home, as they won the Third Division (South) Championship.

DEFEATS – MOST

SOUTHAMPTON'S total of twenty three defeats during the 1971–72 and 1993–94 seasons is the worst in the club's history, yet on neither occasion were the club relegated.

DEFEATS – WORST

THE Saints' worst defeat in the Football League is 8–0, a scoreline inflicted upon them twice. The first occasion was on 28 March 1936 when Tottenham Hotspur beat them at White Hart Lane and then Everton repeated the achievement at Goodison Park on 20 November 1971. The club also had eight goals put past them on 10 November 1951 when they travelled to Bury and lost 8–2.

Southampton have also had seven goals scored against them on five occasions, the last time being on 16 November 1996 when Everton won the Premiership encounter at Goodison Park, 7–1. The club's worst home defeat is 6–0, a scoreline inflicted by Plymouth Argyle on 5 December 1931 and by Brentford on 9 March 1959.

DEFENSIVE RECORDS

SOUTHAMPTON'S best defensive record was established in 1921–22 and helped the club win the Third Division (South) Championship.They conceded just twenty one goals in that campaign and were beaten in only four matches. The Saints' worst defensive record was in 1966–67 when they let in ninety two goals to finish nineteenth in the First Division.

The DELL

GEORGE THOMAS, a partner in a local fish merchant business, paid £10,000 for four and a half acres of land close to the County Ground. The site had a brook running north to south through the middle of it but Thomas had the land levelled, culverted the stream, and set to work on building southern England's most advanced ground.

Because of its origins the ground was known as The Dell, and when it was completed Thomas only charged £250 a year for an eight-year lease.

The Dell was officially opened on 3 September 1898 before a Southern League game against Brighton United which the Saints won 4–1. However, by 1906 when the lease came up for renewal, the club's fortunes were in decline and when Thomas tried to raise their rent to £500 a year, the club had to reject his offer. Thankfully, after a number of lengthy meetings, both parties agreed to a rent of £400.

It was only after the club were admitted to the Football League in 1920 that its future seemed more assured. After winning promotion in 1921–22, £8,000 was spent on extending the ground's East Stand and in April 1926, the club bought the freehold from George Thomas' widow for £26,000.

In 1927 Archibald Leitch was employed to design a new West Stand. It had 4,500 seats on an upper tier, a paddock for 8,500, and was officially opened on 7 January 1928 but after the club's last home game of the following season, a discarded cigarette set fire to litter under the East Stand and by the time the alarm was raised, it had been reduced to a smouldering wreck. The club then had to borrow £10,000 to build a replacement for the start of the 1929–30 season. The Dell then possessed two almost identical stands.

During the Second World War a bomb struck the pitch at the Milton Road End, causing one of the culverts to break and cover the pitch with a couple of feet of water. To make matters worse fire broke out in the West Stand but fortunately the damage was not severe.

After the hostilities, Southampton were one of the first clubs to install floodlights and on 1 October 1951, one of the first competitive football matches played under floodlights was staged at The Dell and a crowd of 13,654 saw the visit of Tottenham Hotspur Reserves for a Combination fixture.

There was little change at The Dell for the next thirty years or so until in 1981 a major rebuilding scheme was undertaken and the whole of the Milton Road terracing was replaced by a two tier terrace, with the uppe tier being triangular in shape. Also at this time a number of relocation stories were going the rounds, but none were pursued until early 1990 when the Taylor Report all but wrecked any hopes of the club having a viable future at The Dell. Unable to ignore the August 1994 all-seater deadline, the club began the conversion of the ground, hoping that its stay at the now much reduced Dell would be as short as possible.

The club would dearly love a joint commitment with Southampton City Council to build a new community stadium on a greenfield site by the M27 at Stoneham, but while the planning battles drag on, the Saints continue to play at The Dell, which celebrates its centenary this year.

DISMISSALS

JACK ANGUS was the first recorded Southampton player to be sent off during a match. It happened in a Hampshire Senior Cup game against Freemantle on 24 February 1894. The first Saints player to be sent off in a Southern League fixture was Arthur Chadwick who received his marching orders in a 2–1 defeat at Sheppy United on 7 January 1899.

Jimmy Moore was the first Southampton player to be dismissed in the Football League during the club's 1–0 home defeat by Grimsby Town on 4 December 1920, although he was later to escape with just a caution.

On 5 November 1977, Southampton played fellow promotion candidates Blackburn Rovers at Ewood Park in a Second Division fixture.

Inconsistent refereeing saw the game boil over and Peter Osgood was ordered off, soon to be followed by Steve Williams. Four other players were booked and the Saints, left with only nine men, lost 2–1.

Micky Adams holds the unenviable record of being the club's first player to be dismissed in the Premier League. He was shown the red card in the Saints' first match in that competition, on 19 August 1992 in a 3–1 defeat at Queen's Park Rangers.

DODD, JASON

THIS outstanding right-back, who has also given first class displays in the centre of defence, joined Southampton from Bath City at the end of the 1988–89 season. He made his league debut for the Saints in a 4–1 win at Queen's Park Rangers in October 1989. He had a good first season but thereafter had to share the number two shirt with Alexei Cherednik and Jeff Kenna.

He played eight times for England at Under–21 level, though many Southampton fans feel he has not received the recognition his all round ability deserves. Dodd can defend, pass the ball well, is better than average in the air and has appeared in more than 250 games for the Saints.

DODGIN, BILL

STARTING his playing career with Huddersfield Town, Bill Dodgin moved to Lincoln City before joining Charlton Athletic, a side he helped rise from the Third to the First Division in the space of two seasons. Surprisingly, he left the Valley for Bristol Rovers before he could taste top-flight football.

After the Eastville club he played for Clapton Orient before arriving at The Dell in the close season of 1939. With the 1939–40 season abandoned after just three games, Dodgin was destined never to play league football again, although he did turn out for the Saints during the war and between 1943 and 1945, was captain.

In January 1946 he was appointed team manager at The Dell, but he did not have much luck. Twice it looked as if the Saints would gain promotion to the First Division but twice they blew it, finishing third in 1947–48 and in April 1949 leading the Second Division table by eight

Bill Dodgin

points, but following an injury to Charlie Wayman, having to be content with third position.

An attractive offer lured Dodgin to Craven Cottage. He spent five years, there during which time he discovered Johnny Haynes, but in October 1953 he was sacked.

He had a short spell with Brentford and coached in Italy before taking charge at Yiewsley. He then joined Bristol Rovers as chief scout before being appointed their manager in April 1969. He produced a number of attacking sides before retiring from the game.

DOMINY, ARTHUR

SOUTHAMPTON were attracted to Arthur Dominy after he had scored fifty goals for Bitterne Guild in 1911–12 and signed him in March 1913. He made his debut a month later and soon established himself as an important member of the Saints' forward line. In 1914–15 he was the leading scorer in the Southern League with thirty goals, including a hat-trick in a 4–3 defeat at Gillingham.

He was employed at the Harland and Wolf shipyard during the war years and, in fact, played for the firm against the Saints in the War League. He managed to score fifty five goals in fifty seven games for Southampton.

When league football resumed in 1919–20, Dominy was again the club's leading scorer and was selected to play for the Southern League against the Irish League, and also attracted bids from a number of First Division clubs.

When the Saints were elected to the Football League, Dominy continued to be a mainstay of the club's attack, forming a formidable strike partnership with Bill Rawlings. An inspirational captain, he took part in many England trial matches but was never capped. The club continued to receive many offers for Dominy's services and resisted them all until

1926 when they reluctantly allowed him to join Everton. He had scored eighty one goals in 257 League and Cup games and sixty five goals in 112 Southern League appearances for the Saints, not to mention his wartime record.

He was a regular in the Everton side in his first season with the club but only played one game in their League Championship winning season of 1927–28 and joined Gillingham where he became the club's leading scorer the following season.

After ending his playing career with Clapton Orient he became a licensee in Southampton. In June 1943, Dominy was given the responsibilities of team manager, but with no training facilities at The Dell he only saw the team on match days. He remained in charge until Bill Dodgin took over in the early part of 1946 and then became landlord of the Southampton Supporters Club.

DOWIE, IAIN

HAVING previously played with St Albans City, Hertford Town and Cheshunt, Iain Dowie joined Luton Town from non-League Hendon in December 1988 and made his Football League debut as a substitute in the new year. He won a regular place the following season, his four goals in the final five matches helping the Hatters avoid relegation to the Second Division on goal difference.

His good form did not go unnoticed at international level either and he made his debut as a substitute for Northern Ireland against Norway in March 1990. A year later he was transferred to West Ham United for £480,000 and scored four goals in the final twelve matches to help the Hammers win promotion to the top flight.

In the early weeks of the 1991–92 season, he was surprisingly sold to Southampton for £500,000 and played a significant role in the Saints' ultimately successful struggle against relegation. Although goal scoring opportunities were rare, all of his nine league goals were either match winners or point savers. He went on to score thirty two goals in 139 League and Cup games for the Saints before joining Crystal Palace in January 1995.

Before the year was out he had rejoined West Ham. The forty four capped Northern Ireland international continued to impress with his all-round commitment, nonstop running and work rate before leaving midway through the 1997–98 season to join Queen's Park Rangers.

DRAKE, TED

ALTHOUGH Ted Drake made his name with Arsenal, it was with Southampton that he was launched on a great career in league and international football.

He began playing for Southampton Gasworks FC and later turned out for Winchester City before joining the Saints in November 1931. He made his debut in a 4–3 win at Swansea Town and over the next few games showed the skills and bravery that were to take him to the top.

After only one season at The Dell, Drake travelled to Highbury for transfer talks but refused to sign and returned to play for the Saints for another season. He had scored twenty goals in thirty three league games in 1932–33 but the following season, his last at The Dell, he netted twenty two goals in twenty seven appearances. He scored a hat-trick on the opening day of the season in a 4–1 home win over Bradford City and although he was sent off in the match at Grimsby, it did not deter Arsenal from paying £6,500 to secure his services in March 1934.

In 1934–35 Drake wrote himself into the Arsenal record books by scoring forty two league goals in forty one games. In this tally were three hat-tricks and four occasions on which he scored four goal. These goals helped Arsenal win the League Championship and gained Drake international recognition when he won the first of only five England caps.

He was one of the most feared centre-forwards in the English game and he netted all seven goals for the Gunners in a 7–1 defeat of Aston Villa in December 1935. Drake was Arsenal's leading league goal scorer in each of his five seasons at the club. During the war he could still be seen in Arsenal colours and scored eighty six goals in 128 games. In all matches for the Gunners he netted 248 goals in 332 games.

After managing Hendon and Reading, he was appointed Chelsea's manager in June 1952 and in 1954–55 led them to the League Championship, thus becoming the first person in Football League history to play for and manage a Division One League Championship-winning combination.

DRAWS

SOUTHAMPTON played their greatest number of drawn league matches in a single season in 1924–25, 1972–73 and 1994–95 when eighteen of their matches ended all square, and their fewest in 1932–33 when only five of their matches were drawn.

The club's highest scoring draw is 5–5 when they entertained Coventry City on 4 May 1982. The Saints also drew 5–5 at home to Plymouth Argyle in the 1945–46 League South competition.

E

EARLY GROUNDS

AFTER playing their first game on the site of the County Bowling Club, next to the County Cricket Ground, the Southampton players tried a pitch on Avenue Road. Unfortunately, a public footpath ran across the middle of it and games sometimes had to be held up to allow pedestrians to cross. The club officials then decided to rent a ground known as the Antelope, where Hampshire County Cricket Club had played from 1863 to 1885.

Southampton enjoyed a number of successful years as leaseholders of the Antelope, but on 1 February 1896 when a record crowd of 12,000 watched the FA Cup tie against Sheffield Wednesday, a barn-like cover collapsed, thus exposing the ground's failings.

Three weeks later, the club were on the move again, this time to the new County Ground on Northlands Road. Hampshire charged the Saints £200 a year, but it was well worth it for in their first year they won the first of many Southern League Championships. In their second season at the County Ground, the club again won the Southern League title and became the first non-League club to reach the semi-finals of the FA Cup. During that run they drew a record gate of 15,000 for the third round replay against Bolton Wanderers.

The club's success led them to look for a ground of their own a and so in 1898, thanks to the enterprise and foresight of local fish merchant George Thomas, the Saints were able to move to The Dell.

ELLERINGTON, BILL

BILL ELLERINGTON came from a footballing family, his father having played for the Saints during the First World War before later playing for Middlesbrough and then Sunderland. He also started his career with Southampton during a war, first playing in the 1940–41 Southern Regional League. He was one of the best full-backs ever to represent the club and went on to appear in sixty one wartime games before making his

Football League debut in the 4–0 home win over Swansea Town on the opening day of the 1946–47 season. Initially, he was competing with Alf Ramsey for the right-back position, but more often than not he was the club's first choice, only losing his place when he caught pneumonia during the Saints visit to Newcastle United later that season.

Ramsey replaced him and went on to win almost immediate international recognition. Ellerington was out of the game for almost a year but when he did recover the Southampton management discovered they had a wealth of talent and experience in the full-back department and let Ramsey join Tottenham Hotspur.

In 1949, Ellerington won two England caps, playing against Norway and France. He went on to appear in 237 League and Cup games for the Saints in ten years with the club before joining Ted Bates' coaching staff.

ELLIOTT, BERNARD

BERNARD or Bryn as he preferred to be known, began his league career with Nottingham Forest, for which he made ten appearances during the 1947–48 season. Unable to win a regular place in Forest's first team line-up, he joined Southampton in October 1949.

After making his debut in a 4–0 defeat at Tottenham Hotspur, the Second Division champions that season, he went on to appear in 251 League and Cup games for the Saints over the next nine seasons, scoring his only goal for the club in a 5–1 home win over Hull City during the relegation season of 1952–53.

Always giving 100 per cent commitment, Elliott played his last game for the Saints in a 5–2 defeat at Bournemouth in February 1958 before having a brief spell with non-League Poole Town.

EUROPEAN CUP WINNERS' CUP

SAINTS first match in this competition saw them comprehensively defeat Olympique Marseilles 4–0 at The Dell with Mick Channon scoring two of the goals. Goalkeeper Ian Turner also played his part, saving a first-half penalty. In the second leg in France, a David Peach goal cancelled out an earlier Marseilles effort but then the French side lost their composure and although they scored a second goal towards the end, the match degenerated into a free-for-all, with Southampton's Hugh Fisher receiving his marching orders. In the second round, Irish club Carrick Rangers were beaten 9–3 on aggregate before the Saints drew top Belgian side, Anderlecht. Despite a rearguard action in Belgium, the Saints lost 2–0 when what looked a perfectly good Mick Channon goal was disallowed for offside.

At The Dell, goals from Peach and MacDougall gave Southampton a 2–0 lead and so levelled the scores, but with just one minute to go Van Der Elst nipped in to score the winner.

EVER-PRESENTS

THERE have been forty six Southampton players who have been ever-present throughout a Football League season. The greatest number of ever-present seasons by a Southampton player is seven by Terry Paine. Next in line is Mick Channon with four.

F

F A CUP

THE Saints first entered the FA Cup competition in 1891–92 and in their first match were drawn away to Warmley, a Bristol club the team of which was made up mainly of bootmakers. Despite the pitch being in a poor state, the Saints won 4–1 and were drawn at home to Reading in the next round.

In what was the first FA Cup match ever to be played in Southampton, the Saints won 7–0 with Jock Fleming scoring a hat-trick. Fleming and McMillan were two members of the 93rd Highlanders, a team Southampton had played in a friendly and were therefor ineligible to play, so the Saints were expelled from the competition after Reading had protested.

In 1897–98, the club reached the semi-final of the FA Cup only to lose 2–0 to Nottingham Forest after the first game had been drawn. Two years later the Saints reached their first FA Cup Final. Some 4,000 Southampton supporters made their way to the Crystal Palace but the club failed to produce anything like their best form and lost 4–0 to Bury.

The Saints reached their second final in 1902 after beating Cup holders Tottenham Hotspur in the first round. Facing Sheffield United at the Crystal Palace, they fell behind to an early goal before Herbert Wood equalised. In the replay, Brown scored for Saints after United had taken the lead and though the Southampton side pressed hard for a winner, Robinson in The Dell club's goal made a costly error and the Cup went to Yorkshire.

The club's third and last appearance in an FA Cup Final was in 1976 when they beat Manchester United 1–0. The game was never a classic, but it was settled when Jim McCalliog threaded a perfect through ball for Bobby Stokes to run on to and slot past the diving Alex Stepney.

F A CUP FINALS

Southampton have appeared in three FA Cup finals, winning the trophy on their last appearance in 1976.

1900	Bury at Crystal Palace	0–4
1902	Sheffield United at Crystal Palace	1–1
1902	Sheffield United at Crystal Palace	1–2
1976	Manchester United at Wembley	1–0

FATHER AND SON

A SOLDIER throughout his football career, Charlie McGibbon scored nineteen goals in twenty eight Southern League outings, including hat-tricks against Luton Town (home 3–2) and Southend United (home 6–2). His son, Doug McGibbon, made his league debut in the last game of the 1938–39 season and, although he played in peacetime, he is best remembered for scoring a double hat-trick in a 7–0 wartime victory over Chelsea, including a goal after just 4.6 seconds of the second-half.

Sam Meston played in 246 Southern League games for the Saints in a variety of positions, winning a record six League Championship medals. His son of the same name broke his leg twice when at The Dell and after struggling to regain fitness, moved on to join Gillingham.

Charlie Sillett was a versatile player who captained the Saints in 1937–38. He played in 175 league games before joining Guildford City. His son Peter played in fifty nine league games before moving on to Chelsea, where he was later capped by England.

FEWEST DEFEATS

DURING Southampton's Third Division (South) Championship winning season of 1921–22, the club went through the programme of forty two matches losing only four games, all of them away from home. The first came in the third game of the season when they lost 2–0 at Gillingham, a side they had beaten by the same score on the opening day of the season. After that the club were unbeaten for the next nineteen games of which thirteen were won before their next defeat, 1–0, at Brentford. The club's two other defeats were also with a 1–0 score line at Swansea Town and Plymouth Argyle.

FIRST DIVISION

SOUTHAMPTON have had two spells in the First Division. They were promoted from the Second Division in 1965–66 and drew their first match in the top flight, 1–1, at home to Manchester City on 20 August 1966, with Terry Paine scoring the Southampton goal.They finished seventh in 1968–69 and 1970–71 and spent the other six seasons battling against relegation until 1973–74, when they failed to beat the drop.

The Saints have been in the top flight ever since they were promoted as runners-up to Bolton Wanderers in 1977–78, and in 1983–84 ended the season as runners-up to Liverpool. They had played fourteen consecutive seasons of First Division football until the new FA Premier League took over.

FIRST LEAGUE MATCH

THE Saints played their first game in the Football League on 28 August 1920 away to Gillingham. Arthur Dominy scored their first goal in the competition, shooting home from an oblique angle to give the club a 1–1 draw. The Southampton team in that historic match was: T Allen, T Parker, F Titmuss, A Shelley, A Campbell, W Turner, J Barratt, A Dominy, W Rawlings, J Moore and F Foxall.

FIRST MATCH

THE club's first match was on 21 November 1885 aganst a team called Freemantle. They were to be Southampton St Mary's main rivals in the early battle to become the top club locally. The Saints won 5–1 with Charles Bromley scoring the first hat-trick for the club and Arthur Fry the other two goals. The Saints side for this first match was: R Ruffell, G Muir, A McDonald, A G Fry, C S Deacon, A Gandy, A A Fry, C Bromley, G Gandy, G McIvor and G Varley;

FISHER, HUGH

GLASGOW-BORN midfield player Hugh Fisher made his league debut for Blackpool against Bolton Wanderers in October 1963 and went on to appear in sixty five League and Cup games for the Bloomfield Road club before joining Southampton for a fee of £35,000 in March 1967.

He made his Saints debut in a 1–0 win at Everton and was outstanding in the club's last eleven games of the season of which they won five to avoid relegation to the Second Division. In October 1971, he broke his leg in the match at Arsenal, ending a sequence of fifty consecutive appearances. The plucky Scot fought his way back to full fitness and was in the starting line up for the visit of Derby County on the opening day of the 1972–73 season.

Hugh Fisher

Although never a prolific goal scorer, he scored eleven goals in 344 League and Cup games, none was more important than his last-minute equaliser against Aston Villa in the FA Cup third round tie at The Dell. It was a priceless goal as the Saints won the replay and went all the way to Wembley where they beat Manchester United 1–0 in the final. Fisher was unlucky to be named substitute for that match, but did not complain. He left The Dell in March 1977 to become player/manager of Southport but later returned to the Southampton area to become a sales representative

FLOODLIGHTS

IN 1951 Simplex floodlights were installed at a cost of £600. The lights, of which there were sixteen, were mounted along both East and West Stands and were used initially for training and friendly matches.

On 1 October 1951, the club staged what is to be believed the first competitive match under floodlights in Britain when a crowd of 13,654 saw the Saints Reserves go down 1–0 to Tottenham Hotspur Reserves in a Football Combination game.

On 5 September 1956, the floodlights at The Dell were used for the first time in a Football League game when they were switched on twenty minutes from the end of the match against Colchester United which the Saints won 2–1.

FLOWERS, TIM

ENGLAND international goalkeeper, Tim Flowers, began his league career with Wolverhampton Wanderers, making his debut at home to Sheffield United in August 1984. Although he conceded two goals in a 2–2 draw, he showed great potential and went on to play in thirty eight league games that season. However, the club was relegated to the Third Division and in 1985–86 relegated yet again, this time to the Fourth Division.

Tim Flowers

Flowers had a spell on loan at Southampton without playing a match before signing for the Saints as Peter Shilton's understudy. He made a less than auspicious start, conceding five goals on his First Division debut at Old Trafford. In his second game against Arsenal he fractured a cheekbone and had two loan spells at Swindon Town before finally breaking into the Southampton side on a regular basis.

After missing just five games between 1989–90 and 1991–92, he was ever-present in 1992–93, when he consistently presented a formidable barrier in the club's first season in the Premier League. He kept twelve clean sheets that season, at the end of which he won his first England cap in a 1–1 draw against a good Brazilian side in the USA Cup match.

A good shot stopper and possessing great concentration, he had played in 234 League and Cup games for the Saints when he was allowed to join Blackburn Rovers for £2.4

million in November 1993. In 1994–95 he helped the Ewood Park club win the Premier League Championship and is a regular member of the England squad, having won ten international caps.

FOOTBALL LEAGUE CUP

THE Saints were not one of the clubs that ignored the inaugural League Cup competition in which they drew their first match 2–2 at Newport County. The replay at The Dell also ended 2–2 before Southampton won the second replay 5–3. That season, the club reached the fifth round before losing 4–2 to Burnley.

One of the most exciting matches in the club's history took place during that run when Derek Reeves scored all Southampton's goals in a 5–4 home win over Leeds United. In the following season the Saints lost to Fourth Division Rochdale, who went all the way to the final before losing over two legs to Norwich City.

There followed a few barren seasons before, in 1968–69, the club equalled their best League Cup placing when they reached the fifth round only to lose 1–0 to Tottenham Hotspur.

In 1978–79 the Saints reached the final of the League Cup for the first time. After beating Birmingham City 5–2 at St Andrews, a Phil Boyer goal was enough to beat Derby County in round three. After a goal-less draw at Reading in the fourth round, goals from Hebberd and Nicholl took the club into round five and a 2–1 victory over Manchester City at The Dell. In the semi-final the Saints drew the first leg against Leeds United at Elland Road 2–2 after being two goals down. In the second leg, a goal by Terry Curran took the Saints through to Wembley and the final against Nottingham Forest. David Peach put Southampton ahead but two goals by Gary Birtles, and another from Tony Woodcock, put the City Ground club 3–1 up before Nick Holmes reduced the arrears in the last minute.

Their best performance in recent years was in 1996–97 when they reached the fifth round only to lose to Second Division Stockport County after a replay.

FORMATION

THE club was formed largely by players from the Deanery FC which had been established by school teachers in 1880. Most of the founders were connected with the young men's association of St Mary's Church. At the inaugural meeting held in November 1885, the club was named Southampton St Mary's and the church's curate was elected president.

FOXALL, FRED

FOLLOWING the outbreak of the First World War, Fred Foxall drifted out of league football with Aston Villa to play for his home town club, Blackheath Town. The Saints noticed his potential and persuaded him to sign for them in 1918. When the club entered the Football League in 1920–21, Foxall was one of three ever-presents but at the end of that campaign, he became involved in controversy by signing for his first club, Aston Villa, without Southampton's permission. The Saints reported him to the FA and he was ordered to re-sign for Southampton.

He continued to give them good service in 1921–22 when they ended the season as champions of the Third Division (South) but in February 1922, the directors announced that Foxall and Barratt would be joining Birmingham with the Blues' Elkes and Getgood moving in the opposite direction.

FULL MEMBERS' CUP

ORIGINALLY it was called the Full Members' Cup because it was open only to First and Second Division clubs. Southampton's first match saw Hull City beaten 2–1 at The Dell with Matt Le Tissier scoring both goals. The Saints lost in the next round at Norwich City 2–1 after extra time, with Jimmy Case scoring Southampton's goal.

G

GABRIEL, JIMMY

JIMMY GABRIEL became one of the most expensive teenagers in British football when he joined Everton from Dundee for £30,000 in March 1960.

A powerhouse of a right-half, he was particularly effective in defence, making him the perfect foil for Brian Harris' adventurous wanderings from left-half. He played a major part in Everton's League Championship success of 1962–63 and was a member of the club's victorious F A Cup side of 1966. The Scottish international went on to play in 301 League and Cup games for the Goodison club before he joined Southampton in the summer of 1967.

He made his debut for the Saints in a 3–0 defeat at Newcastle United on the opening day of the 1967–68 season and in the next five seasons was a regular member of the side. He had played in 215 League and Cup games when in July 1972 he left to join Bournemouth. After some fifty games for the Dean Court club he moved to North America where he played for Seattle Sounders.

He returned to Goodison Park in the summer of 1990 to help manager Colin Harvey look after the first team, later taking over as caretaker boss. Despite all the managerial changes at Everton, Jimmy Gabriel has remained part of the club's coaching set up.

GEORGE, CHARLIE

CHARLIE GEORGE will always be remembered as the long-haired twenty year-old who scored Arsenal's winning goal in the 1971 FA Cup Final, taking the double to Highbury.

He made his first team debut for the Gunners against West Bromwich Albion on the opening day of the 1969–70 season and in that season helped them win the Inter Cities Fairs Cup, their first major honour for seventeen years. A vital member of Arsenal's double-winning side, he then only played in about half of the next four seasons fixtures due to injuries, loss of form and disciplinary reasons. Having become disillusioned with the team he had supported as a boy, he left Highbury in the summer of 1975 to join Derby County. He spent three and a half seasons at the Baseball Ground and won an England cap before signing for Southampton for £400,000 in December 1978.

However, soon after joining the Saints, it was revealed that George had a knee injury and would be out of action for some months. In fact, he did not play his first match for the club until March 1979 at Bolton, but then was substituted in the next and was absent until the opening game of the 1979–80 season.

Although he showed flashes of his old brilliance, he could not be guaranteed a regular first team place and after a loan spell at Nottingham Forest he went to the USA and Hong Kong before coming home to try his luck with Dundee United, Bournemouth and Coventry City.

Charlie George.

GOAL AVERAGE

IN 1949–50, the two Sheffield clubs and Southampton all finished on fifty two points, nine adrift of Second Division champions, Tottenham Hotspur. It was Sheffield Wednesday, with a goal average of 1.398, which joined the White Hart Lane club in the top flight, while Sheffield United (1.387) and Southampton (1.333) were left to look back on missed opportunities, although the Saints won six and drew three of the season's last nine fixtures.

GOALKEEPERS

SOUTHAMPTON FC has almost always been extremely well served by its goalkeepers and most of them have been highly popular with its supporters.

George Clawley, who joined the Saints from Stoke, was one of the club's first goalkeepers. He was an ever-present for two seasons and captained the side in 1897–98. After a spell with Tottenham Hotspur, he returned to The Dell in 1903 and won a Southern League Championship medal.

Jack Robinson was a spectacular 'keeper who won full international honours for England and, during his five years at The Dell, won four Southern League Championship medals.

The club's first goalkeeper in the Football League was Tommy Allen who notched up a record 291 league appearances for a Southampton goalkeeper. He was followed by Bert Scriven who played in 225 league games between the wars.

Eric Martin joined the Saints from Dunfermline in March 1967.There were times during his nine years at The Dell when he was dropped, but he played in 248 league games, a total only bettered by Tommy Allen.

Peter Shilton was arguably the world's best goalkeeper during his stay at The Dell, when he captained the England side in Bryan Robson's absence in the World Cup Finals of 1986.

GOALS

THE most goals Southampton have ever scored in a competitive match was their 14–0 victory over Newbury in an FA Cup first qualifying round match on 13 October 1894, when both Herbert Ward and George Nineham scored hat-tricks.

GOALS – CAREER BEST

THE highest goalscorer in the club's history is Mick Channon who, between seasons 1965–66, 1976–77, 1979–80 and 1981–82, netted 227 goals for the club. The total was made up of 185 in the league, sixteen in the FA Cup, twelve in the Football League Cup, nine in Europe and five in the Texaco Cup.

GOALS – INDIVIDUAL

TWO players have scored five goals in a match for Southampton. The first was Charlie Wayman who netted five in Saints' 6–0 home win over Leicester City on 23 October 1948 and the feat was emulated by Derek Reeves in the fourth round League Cup tie on 5 December 1960 when

Leeds United were beaten 5–4 in one of the most amazing games ever witnessed at The Dell.

GOALS – SEASON

THE club's highest league goal scorer in any one season remains Derek Reeves who scored thirty nine league goals as Southampton won the Third Division championship in 1959–60. He scored four goals against Swindon Town (home 5–1)) and hat-tricks against Southend United (away 4–2) and Mansfield Town (home 5–2). For good measure he also netted six FA Cup goals including four in a 5–1 win at Manchester City.

GOAL SCORING RECORDS

ON 19 January 1895, Joe Rogers caused something of a sensation by scoring ten goals in a 13–0 win over the Wiltshire Regiment in a friendly match. Despite the achievement, he was considered a better full-back than a forward. When the Saints beat Northampton 11–0 on 28 December 1901, Albert Brown scored seven of the goals, whichn is still a record for a league match by a Southampton player.

During the Second World War, Alf Whittingham, a guest player from Bradford City, scored eight goals as Luton Town were beaten 11–0. On 29 December 1945, Doug McGibbon scored a double hat-trick as Chelsea were defeated 7–0 in a Wartime League South game.

When the Saints entertained Leicester City on 23 October 1948, Charlie Wayman scored five goals in a 6–0 win. This is still a Football League record for Southampton to this day.

In 1959–60, when Southampton won the Third Division Championship, Derek Reeves hit thirty nine goals, still a league record for the Saints.

GODFREY, TONY

GOALKEEPER Tony Godfrey joined the Saints in April 1958 but had to wait eight months before making his debut in a 2–1 home win over Stockport County. Over the next seven seasons he shared the goalkeeping duties with Hollowbread, Charles and Reynolds, although in 1961–62, when the Saints finished sixth in the Second Division, he only missed the opening day reversal at Plymouth Argyle. He went on to appear in 149

League and Cup games for the club but when Campbell Forsyth arrived from Kilmarnock in December 1965, it was time for Godfrey to move on.

He joined Aldershot and enjoyed four successful seasons with the Recreation Ground club before moving to Rochdale. Two seasons later he rejoined Aldershot and took his total league appearances for them to 240 before joining non-League Basingstoke.

GOLAC, IVAN

ONE of Southampton's most successful of all foreign imports, Ivan Golac joined the club for £50,000 from Partizan Belgarde in 1978. Under Yugoslavia law in those days, a professional footballer, upon reaching the age of twenty eight, was free to negotiate his own contract and Saints' boss Lawrie McMenemy was quick to offer the hard-tackling Golac a contract at The Dell.

Initially there were problems with the Home Office over a work permit, but these snags were sorted out and Golac made his debut in a 2–2 draw at home to Bolton Wanderers on 22 August 1978.

This Yugoslavian international realised an ambition when he played at Wembley in 1979 in the League Cup Final, which Nottingham Forest won 3–2.

A disagreement over terms caused the popular defender to join Bournemouth on loan during the early stages of the 1982–83 season and after two games on loan with Manchester City, he returned to his homeland to play for

Second Division club, Bjelasica. However, during the latter stages of the 1983–84 season he offered his services to Lawrie McMenemy and returned to The Dell to play in a further twenty four league games. He also had a loan spell along the coast at Portsmouth before leaving the English game.

Golac had appeared in 193 League and Cup games during his two spells with the club. He returned home to coach Partizan and then the national team. On his return to these shores he managed Torquay United before succeeding Jim McLean as manager of Dundee United, a post he held until March 1995.

GOSS, GEORGE

GEORGE GOSS served in the Royal Navy during the First World War and played for naval sides from 1916 until he left the services to join the staff at The Dell as assistant secretary in 1921.

When Ernest Arnfield retired, Goss succeeded him. In thirteen years service he worked under three managers – McIntyre, Chadwick and Kay – and when Kay resigned at the end of the 1935–36 season, he took on the job of manager and secretary. His appointment was seen only as temporary, until the club found a suitable replacement in Tom Parker in March 1937. Goss stayed on until the end of the season and then left to run the Railway Hotel at St Denys. In 1939 he took command of a minesweeper and later emigrated to Australia.

GUEST PLAYERS

THE guest system was used by all clubs during the two wars. Although at times it was abused almost beyond belief – in that some sides that opposed the Saints had ten or eleven guests – it normally worked sensibly and effectively to the benefit of players, clubs and supporters alike.

The most distinguished players to 'guest' for Southampton were Leslie Compton and Eddie Hapgood (Arsenal); Tom Finney (Preston North End) and Jackie Stamps (Derby County), yet it was Bradford City's Alf Whittingham who scored eight of Southampton's goals in an 11–0 home win over Luton Town on 16 January 1943.

H

HAINES, WILLIE

WILLIAM WYNDHAM PRETORIA HAINES began his league career with Portsmouth, scoring on his debut in a 4–1 win over Swindon Town in March 1923. The following season, the Fratton Park club won the Third Division (South) Championship with Haines scoring twenty eight goals in thirty games, including three hat-tricks against Exeter City (home 4–0); Aberdare Athletic (home 4–0) and Norwich City (home 4–0). He continued to score on a regular basis for Pompey and in 1926–27, when the club won promotion to the First Division, he scored forty goals in forty two games, including three hat-tricks and four goals in a 5–1 defeat of Preston North End.

He had scored 129 goals in 159 games when in May 1928 he joined Southampton.

Haines based his game and his shooting on placement rather than force and would often take penalties without a run-up. He made his debut with Southampton in a 2–2 draw at Hull City on the opening day of the 1928–29 season, going on to be the club's top scorer with sixteen goals in twenty seven games, including four in the 8–2 victory over Blackpool at The Dell on 3 November 1928. He continued to score with great regularity over the next couple of seasons but injuries reduced his number of outings and in 1932 after netting forty seven goals in seventy one League and Cup games, he left The Dell to play non-League football for Weymouth.

HARKUS, GEORGE

GEORGE HARKUS joined Southampton from Aston Villa in the summer of 1921 but did not make his first team debut until January 1924 when the Saints beat Barnsley 6–0. He soon established himself in the Southampton side and in 1926–27 was appointed club captain. That season his strong leadership helped the club to a good start and by the turn of the year the

Saints were just two points behind the leaders and promotion looking a distinct possibility. Unfortunately, in spite of Harkus' efforts, the Saints fell away and ended the campaign in mid-table.

In 1930 he decided to retire and became a publican, although he continued to keep fit by turning out for New Milton FC. In February 1932 he returned to The Dell to play in two matches as Saints underwent an injury crisis. The last of his 234 League and Cup games for the club saw them lose 3–0 at home to Bradford. Harkus then went to play on the continent before serving as a flight lieutenant in the Royal Air Force in the Second World War.

HARRISON, FRED

ONE of the best centre-forwards the club has ever produced, Fred Harrison was discovered in the local parks playing for Fitzhugh Rovers in the Southampton Junior League.

He made a goalscoring debut in a 2–2 draw at Portsmouth in October 1901 but it was not until the following season that his ability to score goals came to the fore. In thirteen games in that 1902–03 season, he scored seventeen goals, including five goals in the matches against Wellingborough Town (home 5–0) and Northampton Town (home 7–0) as the Saints won the Southern League Championship. The club retained the title the following season with Harrison netting twenty seven goals in thirty two games, including hat-tricks against Northampton Town (home 5–1) and Bristol Rovers (home 6–1).

Not surprisingly, he was the subject of many large offers from First Division clubs, but the Southampton board rejected these overtures. In 1904 he was given an England trial but unfortunately he was played out of position and failed to impress.

Eventually in 1907, after Harrison had scored eighty eight goals in 166 League and Cup games, the club reluctantly sold him to Fulham for £1,000. He later went on to play for West Ham United and Bristol City.

HAT-TRICK HEROES

THE first hat-trick for the club was scored by Charles Bromley in the Saints' first game, a 5–1 victory over Freemantle in November 1885.

Watty Keay, who scored the Saints' first goal at The Dell, also scored the club's first hat-trick in the Southern League when on 21 December 1895, Reading were beaten 5–0.

The scorer of the club's first hat-trick in the Football League was Arthur Dominy on 21 January 1921 as Watford were defeated 4–1 at The Dell.

On 15 February 1936, both Vic Watson and Arthur Holt scored hat-tricks in a 7–2 home win over Nottingham Forest in a Second Division match. This feat was repeated on 21 November 1964 when Martin Chivers and George O'Brien netted three goals apiece in a 6–1 win over Rotherham United. On 9 December 1945, Southampton beat Chelsea at The Dell 7–0 and Doug McGibbon scored a double hat-trick.

One of the fastest hat-tricks scored for Southampton was by George Kirby in the 6–1 home win over Charlton Athletic on the opening day of the 1963–64 season, when he hit home three goals in the first fifteen minutes of the game.

Bill Rawlings, who hit three hat-tricks in seasons 1921–22, 1923–24 and 1926–27, holds the record for the most hat-tricks for the club with ten in the Football League and another two in the Southern League.

The only player to score a hat-trick on his Football League debut for the Saints is Colin Clarke. He netted three goals in the 5–1 home win over Queen's Park Rangers on 23 August 1986.

On 9 April 1988, Alan Shearer scored a hat-trick in Southampton's 4–2 win over Arsenal at The Dell to become the youngest player in the top flight to achieve such a feat. He was seventeen years 240 days old. It was his first full appearance after two outings as a substitute in the league side.

HOLLYWOOD, DENNIS

THIS tough-tackling competitive full-back worked his way up through the club's junior sides to make his first team debut in a 1–0 home win over Preston North End in October 1962. It was towards the end of the 1963–64 season when he won a regular place in the Southampton side and over the next ten seasons he gained a reputation as one of the league's most feared defenders.

In 1965 the Govan-born player won Under–23 honours for Scotland when he played against England and although he did not progress any further at international level, he went on to serve the Saints well, appearing in 262 League and Cup games.

In the summer of 1972 he left The Dell to join Blackpool but was unable to break into the Bloomfield Road club's first team. He returned to Southampton to work in the docks.

HOLMES, NICK

THIS naturally left-sided player made his debut for the Saints in a 1–0 defeat at Arsenal in March 1974. As he is able to play in a variety of positions, Holmes wore seven different numbers on his shirts while playing at full-back, in midfield, at centre-half, or towards the end of his career, as sweeper.

Nick Holmes

He was a member of the Southampton side which won the FA Cup in 1976 and he also played and scored one of the goals in their 3–2 League Cup final defeat by Nottingham Forest in 1979.

He was selected for the England Under–23 side but had to withdraw from the game owing to an injury.

Holmes went on to appear in 527 League and Cup games for the club, more than anyone else except Terry Paine and Mick Channon. In 1986 the club recognised his great loyalty by awarding him a Testimonial match against John Mortimore's Benfica side. Holmes scored one of Southampton's goals in a 4-1 win over the Portuguese champions.

At the end of the 1986–87 season he was given a free transfer but he was suffering from a serious pelvic injury and had to announce his retirement from league football.

HOLT, ARTHUR

AFTER representing Southampton Schoolboys, Arthur Holt played for Bitterne Congregationals in the Church League before joining Totton. His outstanding performances for the Hampshire League side led to him signing for Southampton in 1932.

He made his debut for the Saints in a 2–1 win against Manchester United at Old Trafford in January 1933. Although more of a scheming inside-forward, he did score a hat-trick for the club in 1935–36 when he netted three goals in a 7–2 home win over Nottingham Forest. He stayed with the Saints throughout the 1930s, scoring forty seven goals in 214 League and Cup games.

Holt also played county cricket for Hampshire between 1935 and 1948, scoring 2,853 runs at an average of 22.46. He later became the county's coach before opening a sports shop in the city.

HOME MATCHES

SOUTHAMPTON'S best home win is the 14–0 FA Cup first qualifying round match against Newbury on 13 October 1894. In the Football League the club's best home win is 9–3 against Wolverhampton Wanderers on 18 September 1965. The Saints have netted eight goals on three occasions – against Northampton Town (8–0 in 1921–22); Blackpool (8–2 in 1928–29) and Coventry City (8–2 in 1983–84).

HOME SEASONS

SOUTHAMPTON have gone through a complete league season with an undefeated home record on just one occasion. It was in 1921–22 when they won the Third Division (South) championship. The club's highest number of home wins is nineteen, achieved in 1959–60 from twenty three matches when winning the Third Division championship.

HONOURS

THE major honours achieved by the club are: F.A.Cup Winners, 1975–76; Third Division (South) Champions 1921–22; Third Division Champions, 1959–60

HORNE, BARRY

WHILE playing as a part-timer for Rhyl in the Northern Premier League. Narry Horne completed a chemistry degreee at Liverpool University. He was a late starter in league football, signing for Fourth Division Wrexham and making his debut at Swindon Town in August 1984. He showed great promise in his three years at the Racecourse Ground and it came as no surprise when he joined Portsmouth in the summer of 1987.

Within a month of his arrival at Fratton Park he made his first appearance for the Welsh national side and since then has gone on to win fifty nine caps. He had made seventy nine first team appearances for Pompey when Saints' manager Chris Nicholl, looking to strengthen his midfield, brought the Welshman to The Dell for £700,000 – the club's most expensive signing. He quickly settled down in the side and apart from a spell out when he was injured at the end of 1989, he rarely missed a match.

Horne had played in 144 League and Cup games for the Saints when in July 1992 he was snapped up by Everton. He made 148 first team appearances for the Goodison club before Birmingham City paid £250,000 to secure his services at the end of the 1995–96 season.

HOSKINS, JOHN

THE nephew of Bert Hoskins who played for Saints between 1906 and 1908 and later managed Wolverhampton Wanderers, he joined the club from Winchester City where he had impressed as a left-winger.

He played his first match for the Saints in a 3–0 defeat at Blackburn Rovers in December 1952 but then scored the equalising goal in a 2–2 home draw against Nottingham Forest. In the next seven seasons he scored sixty seven goals in 235 League and Cup games with 1957–58 being his best season when he netted eighteen goals in thirty seven league appearances, including a hat-trick in a 5–1 home win over Gillingham. In 1959 he left The Dell and joined Swindon Town but after making just ten league appearances for the County Ground club, he entered non-League football with then Southern League club, Cambridge United.

HOUGH, TED

FULL-BACK Ted Hough joined Southampton from Walsall in 1921 for the most unusual transfer fee of fifty two pints of beer. That was apparently the size of the round that one of the Southampton directors had to stand the Walsall management before they would agree to Hough signing for the Saints.

He made his debut in a 1–0 home win over Aberdare Athletic on 17 April 1922 and although he never held down a permanent position with the club, he gave them ten years dependable service, making 184 League and Cup Appearances. At the end of the 1930–31 season he joined rivals Portsmouth, but after just one game, he moved to Bristol Rovers, where he ended his career.

HUNDRED GOALS

SOUTHAMPTON have scored 100 league goals or more in a season on three occasions. The highest total is 112 goals, scored in 1957–58 when they finished sixth in the Third Division (South). In 1959–60 they scored 106 goals in winning the Third Division championship and in 1963–64, they scored exactly 100 goals when finishing fifth in the Second Division.

HUXFORD, CLIFF

THIS strong-tackling half-back arrived at The Dell from Chelsea in the summer of 1959 and played his first game for the club in a 2–2 home draw against Norwich City on the opening day of Saints' Third Division championship-winning season of 1959–60. Huxford was one of four ever-presents that season and was soon appointed Saints' captain, leading by example on and off the pitch.

An ever-present again in seasons 1961–62 and 1963–64, he was an important member of the side that gained promotion to the First Division in 1965–66 after the Saints had finished runners-up to Manchester City. However, after coming on as a substitute for Tony Knapp at Blackpool, he only started one First Division game, that a 4-1 defeat at Sheffield Wednesday before leaving The Dell to join Exeter City.

I

INTER–CITIES FAIRS CUP

IN spite of losing their first European match 1–0 at Rosenborg, goals from Ron Davies and Terry Paine in the home leg took the Saints into the second round. After an exciting 3–3 draw at Vitoria Guimaraes, the Saints ran away with the second leg to win 8–4 on aggregate.

In round three Southampton travelled to St James' Park to play Newcastle United. The Saints played well to earn a goal-less draw and were favourites to win the second leg at The Dell.

A header in the first half from Mick Channon put the Saints ahead and Ron Davies almost made it 2–0 just ten minutes from time when his header crashed against the crossbar. Then with only six minutes remaining, 'Pop' Robson levelled the scores and the Magpies went through on the away goals rule.

Terry Paine.

INTERNATIONAL MATCH

ON 9 March 1901 the only full international match to be played at The Dell took place when England played Ireland. Southampton provided three players for the game – Jack Robinson, Charles Burgess Fry and Arthur Turner all playing for England in a 3–0 win for the home team.

INTERNATIONAL PLAYERS

SOUTHAMPTON'S most capped player – that is with caps gained while players were registered with the club – is Peter Shilton with forty nine caps. Players who have gained full international honours while at The Dell are:

England	
D Armstrong	2
A Chadwick	2
M Channon	45
W Ellerington	2
T Flowers	1
C B Fry	1
A E Houlker	2
K Keegan	9
A Lee	1
M Le Tissier	8
G Molyneux	4
T Paine	19
T Parker	1
A Ramsey	1
W Rawlings	2
J W Robinson	6
A Shearer	3
P Shilton	49
F Titmuss	2
A Turner	2
D Wallace	1
D Watson	18
S Williams	6
M Wright	16

Scotland	
I Black	1
J Robertson	1
Northern Ireland	
C Clarke	12
I Dowie	20
H Kelly	2
J Magilton	18
C Nicholl	37
R Rowley	4
J Shields	1
Wales	
A Curtis	5
R Davies	23
A Hodgkinson	1
B Horne	23
S G Williams	10
Republic of Ireland	
A Byrne	14
J Dunne	2
A Hayes	1
F Kiernan	3
A McLoughlin	4
T Traynor	8

Southampton's first player to be capped was Jack Robinson who played for England against Wales at Bristol on 20 March 1899.

J

JEFFERIS, FRANK

WHEN he was invited to the Dell for a trial Frank Jefferis was playing for Fordingbridge Turks. After scoring a hat-trick in a reserve match, he was chosen to play in a match against the Corinthians and proceeded to score another three goals. Southampton officials were suitably impressed and persuaded Jefferis to sign professional forms, paying Fordingbridge the princely sum of £5 for his transfer.

He played his first Southern League game for the club in a 1–1 home draw against New Brompton in November 1905 and over the next few seasons went on to score forty eight goals in 184 League and Cup games for the club.

Surprisingly, he was allowed to leave The Dell in 1911 and join Everton, where in 1914–15 he won a League Championship medal. He was capped twice by England shortly after arriving on the First Division scene, playing as a scheming inside-forward against Wales and Scotland in 1912.

He moved to Preston North End in January 1920 and two years later was a member of their beaten FA Cup Final side. In 1923 he was appointed player/coach of Southport and retired in the close season of 1925. Two years later he was forced back into action and played two league games when Southport were short of players. In 1936 he became trainer at Millwall and remained there until his death two years later.

JONES, DAVE

DAVE JONES' career as a footballer was cut short by injury after an England Under–21 cap and a promising start to his club career with Everton and Coventry City.

As a manager he has worked his way up from the bottom. He was with Morecambe, Southport and Mossley before moving to Stockport County,

Dave Jones in pensive managerial mood.

first as coach. In fact, Jones only signed a manager's contract in February 1997 before taking the Edgeley Park club to promotion to the First Division at the end of the 1996–97 season.

Appointed manager of Southampton at the end of June 1997, his first move was to get Matthew Le Tissier to sign a new four year contract. The Southampton manager also signed Chesterfield's Kevin Davies and Carlton Palmer from Leeds United and has been an inspired choice, especially compared to the appointments at one or two bigger clubs in 1997–98.

JORDAN, JOE

JOE JORDAN began his footballing days with Morton before Leeds United paid £15,000 to bring him to Elland Road in October 1970 after he had made just ten league appearances. Within a couple of years he was leading the Yorkshire side's assault on the League Championship. He later played in two European finals before Manchester United paid £350,000 for him.

One of the most feared strikers in the First Division, his strength lay in his ability to unsettle defenders and pressurise goalkeepers. In all he played 125 games for United, scoring forty one goals.

Jordan was a regular choice as Scotland's centre-forward and is the only Scot to have scored in three World Cup Finals.

In 1980 he moved to AC Milan and then Verona, from where he joined Southampton in the summer of 1984. He made his debut at Sunderland in the opening game of the 1984–85 season and although he ended the season as the club's leading scorer, his courageous style of play could not take the Saints any higher than fifth place in the First Division.

Joe Jordan.

In 1985–86, he suffered a series of injuries and after scoring seventeen goals in sixty one League and Cup games, he was transfer listed. In February 1987 he joined Bristol City on a free transfer as player/coach, eventually becoming their manager. He later managed Hearts and Stoke City before returning to take charge at Ashton Gate for a second time. He is now assistant to Northern Ireland manager Lawrie McMenemy.

K

KAY, GEORGE

AFTER playing his early football for Bolton Wanderers, he joined Belfast Distillery. He captained the Irish League XI and became the only Englishman to lead an Irish representative side. After wartime service with the Royal Garrison Artillery, Kay returned to England and signed for West Ham United.

Appointed captain just before the start of the 1922–23 season, he led the Hammers to promotion to the First Division and to the famous 'White Horse' Wembley Final where his former club, Bolton, won 2–0. Kay made 259 appearances for the Hammers and was unlucky never to be capped by England. He had a short spell with Stockport County before joining Luton Town as trainer/coach. In December 1929 he took over as manager but in May 1931, he received a more lucrative offer to take charge at Southampton.

At The Dell, Kay created the club's first nursery side and with it, young players such as Drake, Light and Sillett. He managed to keep the Saints in the Second Division but eventually he was forced to sell his best players in order to survive. Southampton supporters were so angry at the sale of Arnold and Keeping to Fulham that a crowd of only 2,949 attended the club's next home match against Bradford City.

Kay resigned as Southampton manager in May 1936 to take over at Liverpool. He spent fifteen seasons at Anfield, leading the Reds to the first post-war League Championship and to the FA Cup Final of 1950. In February 1951 he was advised to retire on medical advice. Sadly, three years later, he was dead.

KEEGAN, KEVIN

BILL SHANKLY picked up the bargain of the decade when he paid Scunthorpe United just £35,000 for Keegan's services in May 1971. Six years later, Liverpool sold him for £500,000. In between he had inspired the Reds to the European Cup, two UEFA Cups, the FA Cup and three

Superstar Kevin Keegan joined Southampton in 1980 for a fee of £400,000.

league titles. He had also been voted Footballer of the Year and had collected twenty nine caps, even captaining his country. Keegan was without doubt a superstar, articulate and fortcoming as well as being one of the greatest players ever to wear a Liverpool shirt. He set up a formidable goalscoring partnership with John Toshack and in 321 games for Liverpool, he netted 100 goals.

He left Anfield in the summer of 1977 to sign for SV Hamburg. He was equally successful in West Germany helping Hamburg to the Bundesliga title and to the European Cup Final. He was also named European Footballer of the Year in 1978 and 1979.

He joined Southampton in July 1980 for a fee of £400,000 and made his Saints' debut in a 2–0 home win over Manchester City on the opening day of the 1980–81 season. Although he went on to score eleven goals in twenty seven league appearances, the season was something of an anticlimax as he suffered from injuries and was forced to miss many games.

In 1981–82, Keegan was the club's leading scorer with twenty eight goals in forty four League and Cup games and his twenty six league goals saw him end the season as the First Division's top marksman. Keegan was voted PFA Player of the Season but then shocked the club just before the start of the 1982–83 season by announcing that he was to join Newcastle United. He became a folk hero at St James' Park, helping the Magpies back to Division One. Before the new season began, he decided to retire an went to live in Spain.

In February 1992 he was appointed manager of Newcastle United in an effort to save the club from the ignominy of relegation to the Third Division. In 1992–93, with the help of his assistant Terry McDermott, he helped the club take the First Division championship, eight points clear of runners up, West Ham United. In January 1997, Keegan caused consternation on Tyneside when he suddenly resigned as Newcastle manager. After a short spell out of the game he became manager of Second Division Fulham.

KEEPING, MIKE

SIGNED from Milford-on-Sea in December 1920, Mike Keeping developed into one of the best left-backs ever to play for the club.

Fast and with a skillful left foot, he toured Canada with the FA XI in

1926 and on his return, was the club's only ever-present the following season. In 1931 he represented the Football League against the Irish League at Blackpool and his form was such that many expected him to win his first England cap. Unfortunately he went down with appendicitis and missed the rest of the 1931–32 season.

Much to Saints' fans disgust, Keeping and Johnny Arnold were sold to Fulham for £5,000. Both men were still in their prime, Keeping having played in 280 League and Cup games for the Saints.

After the Second World War, he coached Real Madrid, later managing sides in Denmark, Holland, France and North Africa before returning to England in 1959 to take charge of Poole Town in the Southern League.

KENNA, JEFF

IN the summer of 1987 Dublin-born full-back Jeff Kenna joined Southampton as a trainee, turning professional two years later. He had to wait another two years for his Football League debut, coming on as a substitute in the penultimate game of the 1990–91 season away to Derby County.

Before his Saints' debut, he had already been selected three times for the Republic of Ireland Under–21 side. At the beginning of the 1991–92 season he had to play second fiddle to Jason Dodd, but at the turn of the year he regained his place and was a member of the Southampton side that lost 3–2 to Nottingham Forest in the final of the Zenith Data Systems Cup Final.

He went on to appear in 133 first team games for the Saints over the next four seasons before joining Blackburn Rovers for £1.5 million in March 1995.

An enthusiastic defender who is able to get forward and join in attacking movements, he has played more than 100 games for the Ewood Park club and has won seventeen caps at full international level for the Republic of Ireland.

KIRBY, GEORGE

LIVERPOOL-born George Kirby started his professional career with Everton and had a few months with Sheffield Wednesday before joining Plymouth Argyle. Despite a disappointing first season at Home Park, matters improved over the next two years and his goal scoring record was then one of which any self–respecting striker would have been proud. It was certainly enough to attract Southampton's attention, for in the autumn of 1962 they paid £17,000 for Kirby's services and he made his debut on 19 September 1962, scoring the Saints' second goal in a 2–1 home win over Chelsea. When Southampton entertained Middlesbrough on 3 November that season, Kirby scored three goals in four minutes in the Saints 6–0 win. In the opening game of the 1963–64 season he scored four goals in a 6–1 home win over Charlton Athletic including a hat-trick in the first fifteen minutes of the match.

However, after only eighteen months at The Dell in which he scored thirty one goals in seventy three League and Cup games, he left to join Coventry City for £12,000. He went on to play for Swansea, Walsall and Brentford and also had a spell in North America before entering management, first with Halifax Town and then Watford.

KIRKUP, JOE

A PRODUCT of the West Ham United youth policy, Joe Kirkup reprsented the London FA before winning England Youth honours. He was only seventeen when he made his first team debut for the Hammers against Manchester City at Maine Road in December 1958.

The winner of three England Under–23 caps, he missed West Ham's FA Cup Final victory of 1964 but twelve months later played in the club's European Cup Winners' Cup victory at Wembley.

In March 1966, after he had played in 187 first team games for the Upton Park club, he was transferred to Chelsea for £27,000. He came to The Dell in February 1968 as part of the transfer deal that took David Webb in the opposite direction. Making his debut for the Saints in a 3–2 home win over Everton, he went on to play in 185 League and Cup games for the club before leaving The Dell to play in South Africa.

KNAPP, TONY

CENTRE–HALF Tony Knapp joined Southampton from Leicester City in the summer of 1961 for a club record fee of £25,000. Having made eighty six league appearances for the Filbert Street club, he arrived at The Dell as an experienced defender.

He made his debut for the Saints in the opening game of the 1961–62 season, a 2–1 reversal at home to Plymouth Argyle, and went on to appear in 103 consecutive League and Cup games including being ever-present in his first two seasons with the club.

Knapp played in 259 League and Cup games for the Saints before leaving to join Coventry City in 1967. After just eleven league appearances for the Sky Blues he moved to Tranmere Rovers where he ended his league career.

After a brief spell playing for Los Angeles, he returned to these shores to become player/manager of Poole Town. There followed a short spell as Norwich City's reserve team manager before he was appointed full-time manager of the Icelandic national side. Later he managed Iceland on a part–time basis while taking charge of a number of Norwegian clubs.

L

LATE FINISHES

SOUTHAMPTON'S final match of the season against Leicester City at The Dell on 26 May 1947 is the latest finish of any Saints' season.

During the Second World War many curious things occurred, among them the continuance of the 1939–40 season into June. Southampton's last competitive match in that campaign was on 8 June 1940 when they lost 3–1 at home to Charlton Athletic in a Football League South B match.

LEADING GOALSCORERS

SOUTHAMPTON have provided the Football League's divisional leading goal scorer on ten occasions. These are:

1948–49	Charlie Wayman	Division Two	32 goals
1957–58	Derek Reeves*	Division Three(S)	31 goals
1959–60	Derek Reeves	Division Three	39 goals
1964–65	George O'Brien	Division Two	32 goals
1965–66	Martin Chivers	Division Two	30 goals
1966–67	Ron Davies	Division One	37 goals
1967–68	Ron Davies**	Division One	28 goals
1973–74	Mick Channon	Division One	21 goals
1979–80	Phil Boyer	Division One	23 goals
1981–82	Kevin Keegan	Division One	26 goals

* Shared with Sam McCrory (Southend United)
** Shared with George Best (Manchester United)

LEAGUE GOALS – CAREER HIGHEST

MICK CHANNON holds the Southampton record for the most league goals with a career total of 185 in his two spells with the club, from 1966 to 1977 and from 1979 to 1982.

LEAGUE GOALS – LEAST CONCEDED

DURING the 1921–22 season Southampton conceded just twenty one goals in forty two games when winning the Third Division (South) championship.

LEAGUE GOALS – MOST CONCEDED

SOUTHAMPTON conceded ninety two league goals during 1966–67 when they finished nineteenth in the First Division.

LEAGUE GOALS –.MOST INDIVIDUAL

Derek Reeves holds the Southampton record for the most goals in a season with thirty nine scored in 1959–60 when the club won the Third Division Championship.

LEAGUE GOALS – MOST SCORED

SOUTHAMPTON'S highest goals tally in the Football League was during the 1957–58 season when they scored 112 goals in finishing sixth in the Third Division (South).

LEE, BERT

BRIDPORT-born right-half Bert Lee came to The Dell in April 1900 as a trialist, playing for Poole Town. He must have made a good impression for he was engaged before the start of the 1900–01 season and, after making his debut in a 1–0 home win over Reading in October, held his place in the side for the next six seasons.

During that time he appeared in 195 games and was a member of the Saints' side that lost to Sheffield United in the FA Cup Final of 1902. In 1904 he won a full international cap when he played in England's 2–2 draw against Wales at Wrexham.

In the summer of 1906, Lee left The Dell to sign for Dundee and spent five seasons with the Scottish club, captaining them to a Cup Final win over Clyde in 1910. He returned to Southampton in the close season of 1911 and played in a further fifty six first team games for the club before becoming player/trainer in the last season before the First World War.

During the hostilities he served at the front and when football restarted in 1919, he was appointed the club's first team trainer. He held the position until 1935, thus ending a long association with the Saints.

LE TISSIER, MATTHEW

BORN at St Peter Port, Guernsey, Matthew Le Tissier first came to Southampton as an associated schoolboy in September 1984 before graduating as an apprentice the following summer and scoring fifty six goals for the Saints' youth team in 1985–86.

He made his league debut as a substitute at Norwich City in August 1986, two months prior to turning professional and during that season he scored eight League and Cup goals including a hat-trick in a 4–0 win over Leicester City. He was the youngest player to score a hat-trick for the club but he did not win a regular place in the Saints' line up until 1989–90, although he had scored nine goals in twenty one starts during the previous campaign.

In that 1989–90 season he scored twenty goals in thirty five league games and hit another four in Cup competitions. The following season he scored twenty three in all matches, including netting the winning goal on five separate occasions. He had earlier declined an offer to become part of the French international set up, preferring to take his chances with England.

In 1991–92, the Saints changed their playing style under new manager Ian Branfoot and goals became very scarce. Le Tissier played and scored in the Zenith Data Systems Cup Final, his first Wembley appearance, but was on the losing side against Nottingham Forest.

He took over the mantle of the club's leading scorer again in 1992–93, the Saints' first season in the Premier League, with fifteen goals including a hat-trick in a 4–3 defeat at Oldham Athletic, scoring direct from a free kick, then a header and finally a volley. He finally came of age the following season when he scored enough spectacular goals to warrant a one man goal of the year contest and finally winning his first England cap, becoming the first Channel Islander to do.

It was during the 1993–94 season that Le Tissier was dropped from the side for five games. The fans protested angrily and demanded manager

Branfoot's resignation. Le Tissier was reinstated and went on to score twenty five league goals including hat-tricks against Liverpool (home 4–2) and Norwich City (away 5–4).

It seems rather unfair to say that Le Tissier kept Southampton in the Premier League single-handedly – but without him and his goals it is likely that the club would have been relegated.

He continued in 1994–95 to prove himself to be the most gifted Englishman in the Premier League but was consistently overlooked at international level.

The cry of 'Le Tissier for England' was never heard louder than when he scored twice in a 3–2 defeat at Blackburn, including a stupendous thirty five yard effort past former Saints' goalkeeper Tim Flowers.

Matthew Le Tissier

He ended the season with thirty League and Cup goals including all four in a League Cup second round second leg win over Huddersfield Town.

He started the 1995–96 campaign with a hat-trick including two penalties against Nottingham Forest which the Saints lost 4–3 but only managed eleven goals and the club only just avoided the drop. He topped the club's scoring charts again the following season and although in the last few seasons he has not scored as regularly as in previous years, his mid-field vision and passing ability are still of the highest quality.

Having played in more than 450 games for the Saints, he continues to pledge his future to the club as long as they remain in the Premier League.

LITTLEWOODS CUP

see Football League Cup

LOTTERY

AT Southampton on 21 March 1987, the club's centenary society lottery draw for £5,000 was won by Guy Askham, the club's financial director. On the same day Lawrie McMenemy, the club's £4,000 a week manager, won the £500 weekly revival draw.

LOWEST

THE lowest number of goals scored by Southampton in a single Football League season is thirty four in 1995–96. However, that was from a a programme of thirty eight matches. The club's lowest over a forty two match season is thirty nine in 1991–92.

The club's lowest points record in the Football League occurred in 1969–70 when the Saints gained just twenty nine points in finishing nineteenth in the First Division.

M

MACDOUGALL, TED

ONE of the game's most prolific goal scorers, Ted MacDougall, began his league career with York City where he first teamed up successfully with Phil Boyer. In the summer of 1969 he joined Third Division Bournemouth.

On 24 November 1970, in the FA Cup against Oxford, he scored six goals and a year later netted nine in an 11–1 win over Margate. That is still the all-time record. Therefore it is not surprising that all the 'big' clubs sought his talents.

In September 1972, amid much publicity, MacDougall signed for Manchester United for £200,000. Although he had scored 103 goals in 146 outings for the south coast club, paying so much money for a Third Division striker was a gamble for new United manager Frank O'Farrell.

MacDougall looked out of place in the top flight, although to be fair to him he was never given much opportunity to find his feet. After only eighteen games for United he was transferred to West Ham United but was just as unfortunate there.

Ted MacDougall.

He then joined Norwich City where he top scored for three seasons in a row and was capped seven times by Scotland. In 1975–76 he scored eleven goals in a six game spell, including hat-tricks against Aston Villa and Everton to end the season with twenty three league goals.

In August 1976, MacDougall moved to The Dell and made his debut for the Saints in a 1–1 home draw against Nottingham Forest the following month. He ended the season as the club's top scorer with twenty three league goals and in 1977–78 netted fourteen league goals as the club won promotion to the First Division. He had scored forty seven goals in 101 League and Cup games for Southampton when in November 1978 he returned to Bournemouth before ending a long career with Blackpool.

MADDISON, NEIL

THE Darlington-born midfielder joined the club as a fourteen year old associated schoolboy in October 1983, before becoming a trainee on leaving school in the summer of 1986. He later turned professional and made his league debut as a substitute against Tottenham Hotspur in October 1988.

In his first two games of the following season he scored a goal apiece but this form did not accelerate his progress and it was 1992–93 before he won a regular place in the Saints' line up. This came following an injury to Glenn Cockerill and he appeared in thirty seven of the forty two Premier League fixtures. The following season he missed just one game, and in 1994–95 this hard-working midfielder again appeared in the majority of games. He was unfortunate to miss a large part of the 1995–96 season due to injury but made a good comeback to once again be an important member of the Saints' side.

MAGILTON, JIM

NORTHERN IRELAND international midfielder Jim Magilton joined Liverpool as an apprentice in May 1986, but as he was unable to break into the first team, he joined Oxford United for £100,000 in October 1990.

His impressive displays for the Manor Ground club, where he scored thirty nine goals in 167 League and Cup games, led to a number of top flight clubs showing an interest in securing his services.

In February 1994 Southampton paid £600,000 for the Belfast-born Magilton and he made his Saints' debut in the 4–2 home win over Liverpool when Le Tissier netted a hat-trick. The following season he was the club's only ever-present as they moved up eight places in the Premier League to finish tenth.

This skilful midfielder, who has won thirty six caps for Northern Ireland, has now played in more than 150 first team games for the Saints and has scored some valuable goals. There have been occasions when the popular Irishman has been left out, but the side always play better with him, something borne out if one looks at the results when he was absent.

MALLETT, JOE

GATESHEAD-born half-back Joe Mallett began his career with Charlton Athletic in 1935 and made two league appearances for the club from The Valley before joining Queen's Park Rangers just before the outbreak of the Second World War.

In February 1947, the Saints paid £5,000 for his services and he made his debut in a 3–2 win at Plymouth Argyle, scoring the winning goal with just minutes remaining. He soon established himself in the Southampton side and over the next six seasons played in 223 League and Cup games, many of them as captain. The last of these games was against Nottingham Forest on 29 April 1953 when the dependable Mallett was thirty seven years 111 days old.

At the end of the 1953–54 season he joined Leyton Orient before becoming coach at Nottingham Forest.

MANAGERS

THIS is the complete list of Southampton's full time managers with the inclusive dates in which they held office. Biographies of all the managers are included in alphabetical order:

George Swift	1911–1912	George Roughton	1951–1955
James McIntyre	1919–1924	Ted Bates	1955–1973
Arthur Chadwick	1925–1931	Lawrie McMenemy	1973–1985
George Kay	1931–1936	Chris Nicholl	1985–1991
George Goss	1936–1937	Ian Branfoot	1991–1994
Tom Parker	1937–1943	Alan Ball	1994–1995
Arthur Dominy	1943–1946	Dave Merrington	1995–1996
Bill Dodgin	1946–1949	Graeme Souness	1996–1997
Sid Cann	1949–1951	Dave Jones	1997–

MARATHON MATCHES

SOUTHAMPTON have been involved in a number of cup games that have gone to three matches. These were Tottenham Hotspur (FA Cup first round 1901–02); Notts County (FA Cup first round 1902–03); West Ham United (FA Cup fourth round 1922–23); Newport County (League Cup first round 1960–61); Scunthorpe United (League Cup second round 1962–63); Chester (League Cup second round 1972–73); Grimsby Town (FA Cup third round 1977–78) and Queen's Park Rangers (League Cup fourth round 1984–85).

MARKSMEN – LEAGUE

SOUTHAMPTON'S top league goal scorer is Mick Channon who struck 185 league goals during his two spells with the club. Only eight players have hit more than 100 league goals for the club.

1		Mick Channon	185
2		Terry Paine	160
3		Bill Rawlings	156
4		George O'Brien	154
5	=	Eric Day	145
	=	Derek Reeves	145
7		Matthew Le Tissier	140
8		Ron Davies	134
9		Martin Chivers	97
10.		Tommy Mulgrew	90

MARKSMEN – OVERALL

TEN players have hit a century of goals for Southampton. The club's top marksman is Mick Channon. The Century Club consists of:

1	Mick Channon	227
2	Terry Paine	185
3	Matthew Le Tissier	184
4	George O'Brien	176
5	Bill Rawlings	174
6	Derek Reeves	168
7	Eric Day	156
8	Ron Davies	153
9	Martin Chivers	107
10	Tommy Mulgrew	100

MARTIN, ERIC

GOALKEEPER Eric Martin joined the Saints from Dunfermline in March 1967 for a fee of £25,000 at a time when manager Ted Bates was seeking to solve a goalkeeping crisis at the club. The Saints' regular goalkeeper, Campbell Forsyth, had broken a leg in the home game against Liverpool and his replacement, Dave MacLaren, who had conceded nine goals when playing for Wolves against Southampton, was suffering a loss of confidence. Martin's impact was immediate. He made a string of fine saves in a 1–0 win at Everton and in the last eleven games of that 1966–67 season, he turned in a number of memorable performances to help the club stave off relegation.

Although there were times when he was dropped, he was an ever-present in seasons 1971–72 and 1972–73, and he appeared in ninety seven consecutive league games. It was during this stage of his career at The Dell that he was being talked of as a Scottish international. Unfortunately he did not gain international recognition but only Tommy Allen made more appearances as a Saints' goalkeeper.

In 1975 after playing in 288 League and Cup games, he left The Dell to play in the NASL with Washington Diplomats.

McCALLIOG, JIM

WHEN the Glasgow-born inside-forward joined Sheffield Wednesday from Chelsea for £37,500 in October 1965 he became the country's costliest teenager. At the end of that season he had helped the club reach the FA Cup Final and scored the first goal in the 3–2 defeat by Everton. He was capped five times by Scotland and on his international debut scored in a 3–2 win against England at Wembley.

He had scored twenty seven goals in 174 games for the Owls when he became unsettled and joined Wolverhampton Wanderers for £70,000. After scoring thirty four goals in 163 league appearances for the Molineux club, he had a short spell at Manchester United before joining Southampton in February 1975.

The gifted ball player made his debut for the Saints in a 1–1 draw at Oldham Athletic and although never a prolific scorer, netted two vital goals in the club's run to the FA Cup Final in 1976 and was the architect of the goal that helped beat Manchester United. He left The Dell to play in the United States for Chicago before returning to England to end his league career with Lincoln City.

McGRATH, JOHN

A TOUGH centre-half who never shirked a challenge, John McGrath was an amateur with Bolton Wanderers before joining Bury and making his league bow with the Gigg Lane club in 1956. After appearing in 148 league games for Bury he moved to Newcastle United in February 1961 and in eight seasons' loyal service to the Tyneside club, played in 181 League and Cup games.

McGrath joined the Saints for £30,000 in February 1968 and made his debut in a 3–2 home win over Everton. He played in the last fourteen games of the season, of which only three were lost as the club moved five places up the league. He later had three games on loan for Brighton before having played in 188 League and Cup games for the Saints, he hung up his boots to concentrate coaching The Dell youngsters.

John McGrath.

He took his first managerial post at Port Vale and led them to promotion to Division Three in 1982–83 but was sacked the following season with the club at the bottom of the table. After a short spell at Chester, he became Preston North End manager in May 1986.

At Deepdale he helped the club win promotion in 1987–88 and the following season led them to the play offs. After his contract was terminated in January 1990, he took charge at Halifax Town but lost his job after Marine beat them in the FA Cup in November 1992.

McILWAINE, JOHNNY

FALKIRK-born Johnny McIlwaine began his career with his home town club before signing for Portsmouth in 1927. A tall, commanding centre-half, he made sixty two first team appearances for the Fratton Park club and played in the Pompey side that lost to Bolton Wanderers in the FA Cup Final of 1929.

He joined Southampton in 1930 for a club record fee of £2,650 – a transfer record that was to last until after the Second World War – but made a disastrous debut for the Saints in the opening game of the 1930–31 season when the club travelled to Preston North End and lost 5–0.

McIlwaine's first season at The Dell was marred by injury and when he did return to command a regular first team place, it was at centre-forward. After another indifferent season in 1931–32 he had a disagreement with the Southampton board and was placed on the transfer list at £2,500. However, no offers were forthcoming and McIlwaine chose to move to Llanelli. After helping his new club win the Welsh League Championship he returned to play at The Dell, once good relations had been restored. He had a better season in 1934–35 and was appointed captain for the Golden Jubilee season of 1935–36.

During the disruptions at the club the following season McIlwaine became assistant/manager to George Goss and club coach, as well as player and captain. Towards the end of the season he began to feel the pressures and left for Grimsby Town where he became the Mariner's masseur and later their assistant manager.

McINTYRE, JAMES

AS a player, James McIntyre appeared for Walsall, Notts County, Northampton, Reading and Coventry before retiring to work in the Humber car factory. He later spent a season refereeing in the North Warwickshire League before joining Coventry as their assistant trainer. Within a matter of months he became the club's chief trainer, a position he held for seven years before moving to The Dell to become Southampton's trainer in April 1912.

The Saints gradually began to improve their league position but with the outbreak of the First World War he returned to Coventry to work in a munitions factory.

In August 1919 he returned to The Dell as the club's manager and a year later the Saints entered the Football League, narrowly missing promotion in their first season. In 1921–22 they won the Third Division (South) Championship to gain promotion to the Second Division but two years later, McIntyre left the game to run an hotel in Scotland.

Coventry managed to persuade him back as their manager but having achieved little success at Highfield Road, he took over at Fulham. In his first full season, the Cottagers clinched the Southern Section title and the following season just missed out on further promotion. In February 1934 he was sacked following a run of poor results and returned to live in Southampton and work at Follands.

McMENEMY, LAWRIE

LAWRIE MCMENEMY failed to make the grade at Newcastle United and joined his local club, Gateshead, but in 1961 an injury ended his career and he became trainer/coach at the club for the next three years. In 1964 he was appointed manager of Bishop Auckland and transformed them into Northen Premier League champions.

After two years as coach at Sheffield Wednesday he was appointed manager of Doncaster Rovers and in his first season in charge took them to the Championship of the Fourth Division. However, when the Belle Vue club was relegated in 1971, McMenemy was sacked. A week later he was appointed manager of Grimsby Town and, again at the end of his first season in charge, they won the Fourth Division championship.

In the summer of 1973, he accepted an offer to become Ted Bates' assistant manager at The Dell, but six months later he was appointed the club's full time manager. At the end of that season, the Saints were relegated and McMenemy came in for a lot of criticism when they did not bounce straight back, but he did take the club to a shock F A Cup Final victory over Manchester United in 1976.

McMenemy signed a number of experienced professionals and in 1977–78 the Saints won promotion to the First Division and a year later reached the League Cup Final but they lost to Nottingham Forest.

In 1983–84, the Saints enjoyed their best season in the First Division when they finished runners up.

In June 1985, McMenemy moved to Sunderland but had a tough time at Roker Park and in April 1987 he was sacked. After three years out of the game, McMenemy returned as assistant manager to England boss, Graham Taylor, but is now manager of Northern Ireland.

MELIA, JIMMY

JIMMY MELIA joined the Anfield staff in 1953 and made his league debut for Liverpool two years later. Capped at schoolboy and youth level, he eventually won a full England cap in 1963 and gained a second cap later that year as England beat Switzerland 8–1 in Basle with Melia scoring one of the goals. He had scored seventy eight goals in 287 games for the Reds when he lost his place and was transferred to Wolverhampton Wanderers for £55,000.

Eigth months later Ted Bates splashed out £30,000 to bring Melia to The Dell. After making his debut in a 1–0 home defeat by Newcastle United, he went on to play a significant part in the club's promotion to the First Division in 1965–66.

His vast experience helped the Saints avoid relegation during their first season in the top flight, but in November 1968 after scoring twelve goals in 152 League and Cup games, he left The Dell to play for Aldershot, later ending his career with Crewe Alexandra.

He tried his hand at management with the Gresty Road club and then Stockport as well as in the Middle East and the United States. He returned to England and in a brief spell as manager of Brighton, took them to a Wembley Cup Final before going to work in Portugal.

MERRINGTON, DAVE

UNUSUALLY among footballers Dave Merrington trained for the ministry. His playing career was restricted to just Burnley, where he made 121 League and Cup appearances, although he has also been involved with a number of other clubs. Although never quite an automatic choice at Turf Moor, he replaced Colin Waldron as club captain for twelve months before being transferred to Bristol City. Almost immediately he was plagued by tendon trouble and was never able to turn out in a competitive match for his new club, later being appointed as coach. In the summer of 1974 he returned to Burnley as coach, and later on worked with Jimmy Adamson at both Sunderland and Leeds United.

After embarking upon full time vocational training as a church minister he returned to football in 1984 as Youth Development Officer at Southampton, a position he held until he replaced Alan Ball as first team manager in July 1985. After working hard to keep the Saints in the Premiership, he was suddenly dismissed in the summer of 1996, ultimately to make way for the return to the English game of Graeme Souness.

MESTON, SAM

HALF-BACK Sam Meston played his early football for his home town club, Arbroath Victoria, until 1893 when he joined Stoke. Two years later he joined Southampton as part of the Stoke 'invasion' and in the next eleven seasons proved himself to be one of the most influential players to be signed in the club's Southern League days.

The ferocity of his shooting earned him the nickname 'Long Tom' after a cannon that was in regular use in those days. He played his first game for the club at Millwall on the opening day of the 1895–96 season and went on to be one of two ever-presents in that campaign. He was also an ever-present in seasons 1897–98 and 1900–01 when his versatility allowed him to play in six different positions for the club.

He won a record six Southern League Championship medals with the Saints and appeared in two FA Cup Finals.

In 1906, after scoring eighteen goals in 246 games, he moved on to play for Croydon Common before ending his playing days with Salisbury City.

MILK CUP

see Football League Cup

MILLS, MICK

MICK MILLS began his career with Portsmouth but was released when the Fratton Park club abandoned their reserve team. Ipswich Town snapped him up and it was not long before he lined up against Wolverhampton Wanderers for his league debut in 1966. Three years later he became the first player in the Portman Road club's history to make 100 league appearances before his twenty first birthday. In 1973 he was called up for the first of forty two full international appearances for England, later captaining his country.

Mick Mills.

He played in 591 games for the Suffolk club, scoring twenty two goals. The highlights of his Ipswich career included the 1978 FA Cup Final victory over Arsenal and the winning of the UEFA Cup.

In November 1982, Lawrie McMenemy bought him for £50,000 and he made his debut in a 1–1 draw at home to Nottingham Forest. He soon fitted into the Saints style of play and over the next three seasons played in 121 League and Cup games, and in every match in the 1984–85 when the club finished fifth in the First Division.

In the summer of 1985 he moved to Stoke City as player/manager but after a number of mediocre seasons he was replaced by Alan Ball whom he had recently appointed as his assistant. He also managed Colchester United and had a spell as assistant manager at Coventry City.

MILWARD, ALF

BORN at Great Marlow, Alf Milward joined Everton in 1888 from Old Borlasians and Marlow and quickly established himself as a first team regular. He performed with great consistency for Everton between 1888 and 1897 and was rewarded with four full international caps for England. Milward forged an exciting left-wing partnership with Edgar Chadwick, both of them scoring goals with great regularity, and he won two FA Cup winners' medals and a League Championship medal. In 1897 after scoring ninety six goals in 224 League and Cup games, he left Goodison Park to join New Brighton Tower.

Two years later, he signed for Southampton and in two years at The Dell never missed a Southern League game. In his first season with the club, he was the leading scorer with twenty four goals in twenty eight league games, netting two goals in a game on nine occasions. Also that season, he helped the Saints reach the FA Cup Final, scoring two of the goals that helped defeat Millwall 3–0 in the semi-final replay. The following season he was joined by his former Everton team mate, Edgar Chadwick, and between them they scored twenty six goals as the Saints won the Southern League Championship. Milward's contribution was twelve goals, including hat-tricks, in the wins over Luton Town (home 5–0) and Queen's Park Rangers (home 5–1).

In the close season of 1901 he signed for New Brompton before retiring two years later.

MOLYNEUX, GEORGE

ORIGINALLY a soldier, full-back George Molyneux played his early football with the Third Grenadiers before joining South Shore and later Wigan County. In 1898 he signed for Everton but after making forty five appearances in twelve months at Goodison Park, he left to join Southampton.

The quick-tackling defender made his debut for the Saints in a 4–3 win at Luton Town in the opening game of the 1900–01 Southern League season, going on to be one of three ever-presents that season as the club won the League Championship.

He was an important member of the club's run to the FA Cup Final in 1901–02 and his outstanding form won him three England caps while at The Dell, the first against Scotland in 1902. Molyneux was ever-present again in 1903–04 as he won his third Southern League Championship medal in five seasons at The Dell. In 1905 after he had appeared in 159 first team games for the club, he joined Portsmouth, later playing for Southend United and Colchester Town.

MONKOU, KEN

SHORTLY after being signed by Chelsea from Dutch club Feyenoord at the back end of the 1988–89 season, Monkou was refused permission to play in a game for his former club. It was a refusal that may well have saved his life for the plane that he would have been travelling on crashed, killing many of his former team mates.

He made his Chelsea debut in the club's Second Division championship winning side against Stoke City in May 1989 before establishing himself the following season as the club consolidated its position in the First Division. He went on to appear in 109 League and Cup games for the Stamford Bridge club before joining Southampton for £750,000 in the summer of 1992.

Voted Man-of-the-Match in his first three games at The Dell, he continued to impress throughout the club's first season in the Premier League and completely shackled former Saints' favourite, Alan Shearer, when his new club Blackburn Rovers visited The Dell. One of his most important goals for the club was the last minute winner against Norwich City in 1993–94, to give the Saints a 5–4 win at Carrow Road after trailing 3–1.

The following season he suffered a collapsed lung when colliding with David James during a home defeat against Liverpool. Happily the strong Dutch Under–21 international recovered fully and continues to turn in outstanding performances at the heart of the Southampton defence.

MORAN, STEVE

MANAGER Lawrie McMenemy was watching local junior football one Sunday morning when he spotted this talented Croydon-born youngster. He offered the schoolboy a new pair of boots if he was able to score a second half hat-trick. Moran duly obliged and signed professional forms in the summer of 1979 after he had finished his schooling.

He made a goal scoring debut for the Saints as a substitute for Ivan Golac in a 4–1 home win over Manchester City on 19 January 1980. The following season he won a regular place in the Southampton side, linking up well with Channon and Keegan. He ended that 1980–81 campaign as the club's leading scorer with eighteen league goals, many of which were typical pieces of opportunist finishing. The following season, he suffered a severe back injury after scoring nine goals in the first eighteen matches. He needed an operation and was out of first team action for over nine months. On his return, he scored his first hat-trick for the club in a 4–1 home win over Manchester City – coincidentally the same opponents and scoreline of his Southampton debut.

During the 1982–83 season, Moran and Mark Wright were detained by Swedish police following accusations by a young girl – which later turned out to be completely untrue. The following season, Moran was back to his best, scoring twenty one league goals and four in Cup competitions, including a hat-trick in an 8-2 home win over Coventry City.

An England Under–21 international, he netted another hat-trick against Ipswich Town in May 1985 and then his last for the club in October 1985 as Watford were beaten 3–1. In September 1986, Moran, after scoring ninety six goals in 215 League and Cup games, left The Dell to join Leicester City for a fee of £300,000. Playing in a Filbert Street side struggling against relegation and he himself hampered by injuries, he joined Reading a year later before playing for Exeter City and Hull City.

MOST MATCHES

SOUTHAMPTON played their greatest number of matches, sixty one, in 1991–92 season. They were forty two league games, seven FA Cup games, six Football League Cup games and six Zenith Data Systems Cup games. They reached the final at Wembley, only to lose 3–2 to Nottingham Forest.

MULGREW, TOMMY

MOTHERWELL-born forward Tommy Mulgrew began his career with Morton before coming south to join Northampton Town in the summer of 1949. In October 1952 he signed for First Division Newcastle United but failed to impress at St James' Park and in July 1954 he joined the Saints along with Billy Foulkes for a combined fee of £12,000.

He had a remarkable debut, scoring after just fifteen seconds of the Saints' opening match of the 1954–55 season which resulted in a 6–4 home win over Brentford. He showed plenty of promise in that first season at The Dell but it was largely unfulfilled, and he lacked consistency in front of goal. The following season Mulgrew became the first Southampton player for twenty two years to be sent off, receiving his marching orders in the 1–0 home win over Coventry City.

His goal scoring exploits made him hugely popular with the Southampton supporters and in eight seasons at The Dell, he scored 100 goals in 325 League and Cup appearances.

In the summer of 1962, Mulgrew had a disagreement over terms with the Southampton board and left to join Aldershot, appearing for them in 112 league games. After ending his league career at the Recreation Ground he had a short spell with non-League Andover FC.

N

NEUTRAL GROUNDS

Southampton have had to replay on a neutral ground a number of times:

Date	Opponents	Venue	FA Cup	Score
03.02.1902	Tottenham Hotspur	Elm Park	Round 1	2-1
16.02.1903	Notts County	St Andrews	Round 1	1-2
19.03.1923	West Ham United	Villa Park	Round 4	0–1
08.04.1963	Nottingham Forest	Tottenham	Round 6	5–0
16.01.1978	Grimsby Town	Filbert St	Round 3	4–1

The club was also involved in playing two League Cup ties on a neutral ground.

09.10.1962	Scunthorpe United	London Rd	Round 2	0–3
20.09.1973	Chester	Hawthorns	Round 2	2–0

The FA Cup semi-finals were, of course, played on neutral grounds and of their ten appearances in this stage of the competition, four have been at Stamford Bridge, two at White Hart Lane and one each at Bramall Lane, Elm Park, Villa Prk and Highbury. The the replay of 1898 was at Crystal Palace. The Saints' FA Cup final appearances at the Crystal Palace and Wembley also qualify for inclusion as do the club's League Cup Final and Zenith Data Systems Cup Finals at Wembley.

NICHOLL, CHRIS

CHRIS NICHOLL played his first Football League game for Halifax Town after joining the Shaymen from non-League Witton Albion in the summer of 1968. His next move was to Luton Town where he was an important member of a Hatters' defence when they won promotion from the Third Division. He joined Aston Villa in March 1972 for £75,000 and played in the last thirteen games of that season, grabbing an important equalising goal in his second game at Shrewsbury to help Villa win the Third Division championship.

He won two League Cup winners' tankards with Villa, scoring one of the goals that defeated Everton in the third meeting between the two clubs in the 1977 final. vIn 1976, the popular centre-half managed to score all four goals in a 2–2 draw against Leicester City at Filbert Street.

After playing in 250 games for Villa, Nicholl joined Southampton in the summer of 1977 and helped them return to the top flight at the end of his first season. He also appeared for the Saints in the League Cup Final of 1979 and in Europe during the early 1980s. He left The Dell in the close season of 1983 after playing in 226 League and Cup games in six seasons with the club.

Chris Nicholl.

He joined Grimsby Town but two years later returned to The Dell, replacing Lawrie McMenemy. Nicholl lost his job at the end of the 1990–91 season and is now manager of Walsall.

NICKNAMES

IT was during the 1888–89 season that the club's nickname 'Saints' was first used, thanks to a worker at the Ordnance Office. He designed a white shield with a red stripe across it. On the shield were printed the words 'Play Up Saints'. Thousands of the shields were distributed throughout the town and worn in the hatbands of Southampton supporters.

The club also had a less than pleasant nicknames bestowed upon it in the 1970s by Liverpool manager Bill Shankly. Following a particularly bruising encounter between the Saints and his own Liverpool side, he referred to the side from The Dell as the 'Ale House Brawlers', a nickname that stuck for some years.

Many players in the club's history have had nicknames. Willie Naughton, 1895–1898, was affectionately known as 'Chippy'; Fred

Harrison, 1901–1908, was 'Buzzy'; Robert Carter, 1908–1910, was 'Toddler'; and Willie Henderson, 1923–1928, was 'Tishy'.

NON–LEAGUE

SOUTHAMPTON reached the FA Cup Final as a non-League club twice in three years. The Saints were a Southern League club when they reached the 1900 and 1902 finals. They lost both. In 1902 they became only the second, and subsequently one of only four non-League clubs to beat the Cup holders, when they defeated Tottenham Hotspur 2–1 after two drawn games.

Since becoming members of the Football League, the Saints have met non-League opposition in the FA Cup on five occasions with the following results:

Date	Opponents	Venue	Score
07.01.1939	Chelmsford City	Away	1–4
20.11.1954	Barnet	Away	4–1
08.12.1956	Weymouth	Home	3–2
16.11.1957	Walton and Hersham	Away	6–1
15.11.1958	Woking	Home	4–1

O

O'BRIEN, GEORGE

GEORGE O'BRIEN had played in forty three league games for Leeds United when, in July 1959, Southampton signed him for a fee of £10,000. He made his debut for the club in a 2–2 home draw against Norwich City on the opening day of the 1959–60 season and went on to score twenty three goals in forty two games. He formed a formidable goal scoring combination with Derek Reeves who scored thirty nine goals in forty six games as Southampton won the Third Division championship.

In 1960–61 O'Brien was the club's leading scorer with twenty two goals in forty one league games, including all four in a 4–2 home win over Brighton and Hove Albion. The following season he netted twenty eight league goals including a hat-trick in a 4–1 win at Luton Town. In 1962–63 he again headed the club's goal scoring charts with twenty two goals plus another seven in the Saints' run to the FA Cup semi-finals which included a hat-trick in the 5–0 demolition of York City.

Injuries hampered him during the next season but in 1964–65 he returned to score thirty two goals in forty one league games including all four against Charlton Athletic and hat-tricks against Rotherham United (Home 6–1) and Plymouth Argyle (Home 5–0). On 4 September 1965 O'Brien scored four goals for the club for the third time in a 6–2 win over Bury, but in March 1966 he left The Dell to play for Leyton Orient.

O'Brien, who was second only to Charlie Wayman in terms of scoring rate, scored 187 goals in 277 League and Cup games. He was a great favourite at The Dell and he later moved to Aldershot, where he ended his league career.

OLDEST PLAYER

THE oldest player to line up in a Southampton first team is Peter Shilton. He was thirty seven years 233 days old when he played his last game for the club against Coventry City (Away 1–1) on 9 May 1987.

O'NEIL, BRIAN

STARTING his career with Burnley, O'Neil moved quickly through the junior ranks and was a member of both Central League Championship sides of 1961–62 and 1962–63 before making his First Division debut in April 1963 at the age of nineteen. His powerful performances for the Clarets were good enough to bring him to the attention of the international selectors and he represented the Football League in 1965 and won one Under–23 cap for England against Turkey in April 1966.

As Burnley's fortunes began to decline, some of the club's stars sought new horizons. Southampton admired O'Neil to such an extent that they broke their transfer record to sign him for £75,000 in the summer of 1970.

O'Neil made his Saints' debut in a 1–1 draw at home to Manchester City on the opening day of the 1970–71 season, and was one of three ever-presents in that campaign, as the club finished seventh in the First Division and his former club, Burnley, was relegated He was an inspiration and only a bad disciplinary record – he was suspended for nine weeks on one occasion – prevented him from winning full international honours.

Known as the 'Bedlington Terrier', he appeared in 166 League and Cup games for the Saints, scoring eighteen goals but after they were relegated in 1974 he left to play for Third Division Huddersfield Town. He immediately won a first team place but could not prevent the Yorkshire side from being relegated to Division Four for the first time ever. After a year in the basement, he retired from league football to become player/manager of Bideford Town.

OSGOOD, PETER

PETER OSGOOD was a brilliant individualist who graced the English game for a decade. He signed for Chelsea in September 1964 where his tremendous skills made him a great crowd favourite. He could put thousands on the gate at the height of his powers and he was an automatic first team choice at Chelsea until he had public rows with manager Dave Sexton. For the Stamford Bridge club he scored 150 goals in 380 games, including five against Jeunesse Hautcharage in European competition.

Osgood's goal flair was most evident in Cup Finals and he netted against Leeds United (FA Cup) Stoke City (League Cup) and Real Madrid (European Cup Winners' Cup). He was also capped four times by England which was a travesty for a man of his rare talent.

Lawrie McMenemy splashed out a record £275,000 to take him to Southampton, the first in a long line of high profile senior and even wayward stars brought to The Dell.

Peter Osgood.

He made his debut in a disastrous 4–1 defeat at Stoke City in March 1974 and, although he impressed in his early games for the club, he could not prevent them being relegated to the Second Division. He won a second FA Cup winners' medal in 1976 before he had a month's loan spell with Norwich City.

He left The Dell to play for Philadelphia Fury before returning to Chelsea in December 1978 where he ended his league career.

Osgood, who was originally a bricklayer has, since leaving the game, been a Windsor licensee, a coach at holiday camps, a sports promotion manager and, more recently, a Match Day host for Chelsea.

OVERSEAS PLAYERS

ONE of the club's most successful imports was Yugoslav international Ivan Golac who joined the Saints from Partizan Belgrade in 1978. He went on to play in 193 League and Cup games for the club. Another Yugoslav international to play for the club was goalkeeper Ivan Katalinic who joined the Saints from Hajduk Split in 1979.

Other overseas players to have played for Southampton have been Aleksey Cherednik, a Russian international defender who joined the club from Dneproptro and Sergei Gotsmanov another Russian who also arrived in the summer of 1990 from Dynamo Minsk.

Ken Monkou signed for Southampton from Chelsea in August 1992 for a fee of £750,000. The former Feyenoord defender who combines his aerial ability with solid tackling has been a great servant of the club. Also, Ronnie Ekelund, a Danish international had a spell on loan from Barcelona.

When Graeme Souness was appointed Southampton manager in July 1996, he invested £1.4 million in Galatasaray defender Ulrich van Gobbel, £1 million in Eyal Berkovic from Haifa Maccabi and a further £2 million on Norwegians Egil Ostenstad and Claus Lundekvam.

OWN GOALS

ALTHOUGH a number of Southampton players have put through their own goals, the afternoon of 28 March 1925 was a tragic one for Tom Parker. The Saints were playing Sheffield United at Stamford Bridge in the FA Cup semi-final and Parker, in attempting to play the ball out for a corner, sliced it past Tommy Allen to put the Blades ahead. To make matters worse, Parker then missed a second half penalty before being involved in a mix up with goalkeeper Allen to make the Yorkshire club a gift of a second goal.

P Q

PAINE, TERRY

TERRY PAINE began his football career with his home club, Winchester, then managed by former Southampton forward Harry Osman. He recommended the young Paine to Saints' manager, Ted Bates, and in August 1956 he was added to the club's playing staff.

He made his Southampton debut in a 3–3 home draw against Brentford on 16 March 1957 and on his next appearance scored in Saints' 1–1 draw at Aldershot on his eighteenth birthday. Alternating from left to right wing, he was ever-present in 1958–59 and again in 1959–60 when the club won the Third Division championship. That season Paine was irrepressible and was rewarded with his first England Under–23 cap when he played against Holland.

In 1960–61, the club's first season back in the Second Division, Paine was again ever-present and scored eighteen league goals, plus another seven in Cup competitions. On 18 November 1961 he missed the home match against Sunderland after appearing in 160 consecutive league games from 22 March 1958 but in 1962–63 was again ever-present.

In 1963 he won the first of nineteen full international caps for England when he played against Czechoslovakia and later that year scored a hat-trick at Wembley in an 8–3 win over Northern Ireland to become the first outside-right since Stanley Matthews in 1937 to score three goals for England. He was part of Alf Ramsey's plans for the 1966 World Cup, though he only played in the 2–0 win over Mexico, a match in which he was injured. It was Paine's last international appearance, all of his caps being won when he was a Second Division player.

In 1963–64, Paine finished the season as Saints' joint leading league scorer with twenty one goals including hat-tricks against Rotherham United (away 3–2) and Derby County (home 6–4). He was an important member of the Southampton side that won promotion to the First Division in 1965–66, and was ever–present the following season in the top flight when his endless stream of pinpoint crosses brought Ron

Davies thirty seven goals in forty one league games. The following season saw Paine used in more of a midfield role and there were even calls for him to be reinstated in the England side as his passing skills began to unlock even the tightest of First Division defences.

Staying free from injury, Paine broke both the club appearance and goal scoring records, playing in 801 League and Cup games and scoring 183 goals.

In 1974 he left The Dell to join Hereford United, playing in another 106 games and so appear in more league games than any other player. When he finally hung up his boots, he went into management with Cheltenham Town. He was awarded the MBE for his services to football and he now works as a football coach in South Africa.

PARKER, TOM

AFTER playing with Sholing Rangers, Sholing Athletic and St Mark's in the war league, Tom Parker joined Southampton in 1918 and during the following season was an ever-present in the South Hants War League.

Parker signed professional forms in May 1919 and in his first season in the Southern League not only developed a splendid partnership with Fred Titmuss but also scored ten times from the penalty spot. Parker was a quality full-back, strong in the tackle and a good distributor of the ball. In 1925 he was capped by England and starred in a 3–2 win over France in Paris. Not surprisingly, he was the subject of a number of big offers from the top clubs and in March 1926 after appearing in 2,754 first team games, he joined Arsenal for £3,250.

The Gunners manager, Herbert Chapman, realised that Parker was a born leader and made him captain. He made his debut for the Highbury club against Blackburn Rovers in April 1926, this starting a run of 150 consecutive first team games for the club. After appearing in the club's FA Cup Final of 1927 he made history by becoming the first Arsenal captain to hold aloft the FA Cup at Wembley after they had beaten Huddersfield Town in 1930. He also led Arsenal to their first League Championship in 1930–31 and to a second FA Cup Final against Newcastle United in 1932. He was granted a free transfer in March 1933 and became manager of Norwich City.

In February 1937 he joined managerless Southampton and over the next two seasons spent £9,000 on new players, including signing two future managers, Bill Dodgin and Ted Bates. Having built a settled side, his planning was wasted with the outbreak of the Second World War and after continuing as secretary/manager until 1943 he left to work for the Ministry of Transport.

He later had a second spell as manager of Norwich City before returning to Southampton to become chief scout.

PEACH, DAVID

THE Bedford-born full-back began his career with Gillingham and had made 187 league appearances for the Kent club when he became Lawrie McMenemy's first signing in January 1974.

David Peach.

He made his debut for the Saints in midfield as a substitute for Hugh Fisher in a 2–2 home draw against Queen's Park Rangers. He was quickly moved to left-back, where he was both quick-moving and imaginative. He was also the club's penalty taker and had a high success rate, the one he converted against Crystal Palace in the FA Cup semi-final at Stamford Bridge taking the Saints to Wembley. An FA Cup winners' medal in 1976 was quickly followed by international recognition at Under–21 and B levels and in June 1977 he toured South America as Trevor Cherry's deputy with the full England squad.

He had played in 267 League and Cup games for the Saints when in March 1980 he left The Dell to join Swindon Town for £150,000. Two years later he joined Orient, where he became the only player in the Football League to have played on every league ground.

PENALTIES

IN 1919, when Southampton played Northampton Town, right-back and captain Tom Parker missed a penalty in the first half. Later in the game he took over in goal from the injured Saints' goalkeeper and duly made amends by saving a Cobblers' spot kick.

When Southampton played Sheffield United at Stamford Bridge in the semi-final of the FA Cup in 1925, it was Parker who was involved in another penalty incident. Having already put the Blades ahead by slicing the ball past his own goalkeeper, he drove a penalty straight at the United goalkeeper before also being responsible for the Yorkshire side's second goal in a 2–0 defeat for the Saints.

PITCH

THE Dell pitch measures 110 yards by 72 yards.

PLASTIC

THERE have been four Football League clubs that replaced their normal grass playing pitches with artificial surfaces at one stage or another. Queen's Park Rangers were the first in 1981, followed by Luton Town, Oldham Athletic and Preston North End.

The Saints never played on the Boundary Park or Deepdale plastic and though their record on Luton's Kenilworth Road artificial surface included 7–0 and 6–1 defeats, their performances on Queen's Park Rangers' Loftus Road plastic saw them win three of the six encounters, including a 4–0 victory on 2 February 1985.

POINTS

UNDER the three points for a win system, which was introduced in 1981–82, Southampton's best points tally is the seventy seven from forty two matches in 1983–84 when they finished runners up in the First Division.

The club's best points tally under the old two points for a win system was sixty one points from forty two matches in 1921–22 when it won the Third Division (South) Championship and from forty six matches in 1959–60 when they won the Third Division Championship. Under the present system, these would have netted the club eighty four and eighty seven points respectively.

The worst record, under either system, was the twenty nine points secured in 1969–70 when the club finished nineteenth in the First Division.

PORTSMOUTH

SOUTHAMPTON'S arch rivals are Portsmouth and the two clubs first met on 5 September 1889 at Fratton Park when the home side won 2–0. The two clubs met many times in a variety of competitions before they both entered the Third Division of the Football League. In 1915–16 Pompey won 7–0 with Frank Stringfellow netting a hat-trick. In the South Hants War League of 1918–19 the clubs met four times, Portsmouth winning two of the meetings and one ending all square before Southampton won the fourth, 9–1.

Their first meeting in the Football League was on 11 September 1920 when Southampton won 2–0 at The Dell with goals from Parker and Moore. The Saints completed the double a week later, winning 1–0 at Fratton Park, courtesy of a Bill Rawlings goal. In fact, Pompey did not win a league game against the Saints until 5 September 1925, the seventh time the clubs had met in the competition.

After the 1926–27 season, the clubs did not meet again for thirty four years but when they did the Saints won their home match 5–1. When the two clubs met at Fratton Park on 5 February 1966, Southampton won 5–2 with Norman Dean grabbing a hat-trick.

The clubs last met in 1987–88, the only time they have played each other in the top flight. They shared the points in a 2–2 draw at Fratton Park, but goals from Barry Horne and Terry Connor gave Pompey a 2–0 victory at The Dell.

POSTPONED

THE Southampton v York City third round FA Cup tie was postponed nine times before the Saints, with goals from O'Brien (3), Burnside and Wimshurst, won 5–0 on 13 February 1963.

PREMIER LEAGUE

IN 1992–93, the club's first season in the Premier League, the writing appeared to be on the wall early in the campaign as they slumped into the relegation zone. But after Christmas the Saints put together significant string of results which took them out of immediate danger. Despite a surge up the table, a disappointing run later on sent the side tumbling back into relegation territory and they ended the season in eighteenth place. To make matters worse, they collected the highest number of Premier League bookings – thirty five, with five dismissals. It earned them a £25,000 suspended fine from the FA before the start of the 1993–94 season.

It was a season when Matt Le Tissier came of age, scoring twenty five goals, but despite his outstanding contribution the first nine games only brought one win. In fact, although the club again finished eighteenth, survival was only secured on the last day of the season after a 3–3 draw at West Ham United.

In 1994–95 Bruce Grobbelaar saved an Alan Shearer penalty on his debut in a 1–1 draw against Blackburn Rovers on the opening day of the season but with only one win in six games, it was a sorry start. The Saints then began to pick up and although their safety was only secured on the final day of the season again, with a point at home to Leicester City, they ended the campaign in tenth place.

With Alan Ball leaving to join Manchester City in the 1995 close season, Dave Merrington was given the job of improving on last season's position. A Matt Le Tissier hat-trick on the opening day of the season gave them a perfect start, but the 4–3 defeat of Nottingham Forest was one of only two occasions when the Saints scored more than twice in a league game. Midway through the season it seemed as if Southampton were on the verge of the drop after just two wins in sixteen games, but they not only helped their own survival chances when they beat Manchester United 3–1 but threw the title race wide open. Again they needed a point at home to Wimbledon on the final day of the season to stay up – a goal-less draw was duly achieved.

In 1996–97, under new manager Graeme Souness, the club failed to win any of their first seven games but a 6–3 drubbing of Manchester United helped it move out of the relegation zone. A 7–1 beating at Everton was the first of five successive defeats but after that results picked up somewhat and a seven game unbeaten run towards the end of the season ensured that the club retained its Premier League status.

PROMOTION

SOUTHAMPTON have been promoted on three occasions, first in 1959–60 when they won the Third Division championship. They played some superb football and scored 106 goals with Derek Reeves netting thirty nine, still a league record for the Saints. They beat Shrewsbury Town 6–3, Swindon Town 5–1, Coventry City 5–1, Accrington Stanley 5–1 and Mansfield Town 5–2 and scored four goals in a match on five occasions.

Saints were next promoted in 1965–66 when they finished the season as runners up to Manchester City. Wolverhamptomn Wanderers were beaten 9–3 with Martin Chivers, top scorer with thirty goals, netting four. A goal-less draw at Maine Road against champions Manchester City ensured that at long last First Division football was coming to The Dell.

After being relegated in 1973–74, the Saints spent four seasons in the Second Division before experiencing their third and final promotion in 1977–78 when they finished runners up to Bolton Wanderers. In the final game of the season, Southampton entertained Tottenham Hotspur and had to win to overhaul the Wanderers and become champions. Spurs, meanwhile, needed a point to beat Brighton for the third promotion place. The game ended goal-less and both clubs joined Bolton in the top flight.

QUICKEST GOALS

IT is an impossible task to state accurately who is the club's quickest goalscorer. Doug McGibbon had the ball in the Chelsea net after allegedly only 4.6 seconds of the second half starting in Southampton's 7–0 League South wartime win on 29 December 1945.

R

RAMSEY, ALF

ONE of the most famous managers of all time who took England to their World Cup triumph over West Germany in 1966.

As a player, he was a strong, polished and distinguished defender who joined Portsmouth as an amateur in 1942 before moving to The Dell a year later. Ramsey was stationed with the army near Southampton and had impressed Saints' secretary, Mr Sarjantson, when he played in a trial game. He made his league debut for the Saints in a 5–1 home win over Plymouth Argyle in October 1946 but only won a place on a regular basis after Bill Ellerington went down with pneumonia. The following season, Ramsey was the club's only ever-present as it finished third in the Second Division and in 1948 was capped by England against Switzerland in a 6–0 win at Highbury. In 1948–49 he was injured in a friendly at Plymouth and when he recovered he found that he could not oust Ellerington from the side. He asked for a transfer and in May 1949 he joined Tottenham Hotspur for £21,000, a record fee for a full-back.

Virtually an ever-present in the teams that won the Second Division and Football League titles in 1950 and 1951, he was very accurate with penalties and free kicks and developed into a great reader of the game.

After he hung up his boots in 1955 he became manager of Ipswich

Town and led them to the Third Division (South) title in 1956–57, the Second Division Championship in 1960–61 and the First Division title in 1961–62.

In January 1963 he was appointed as the first full-time manager of England and in 1966 when playing on home territory took the World Cup for the first and only time. In May 1974, after England had failed to qualify for the finals of that year's World Cup competition, he was sacked.

In September 1977, Sir Alf was appointed manager of Birmingham City,but only held office for six months before being forced to relinquish the position due to ill health.

RAPID SCORING

ON 18 September 1965, the Saints entertained Wolverhampton Wanderers at The Dell. After only thirty five seconds a Tony Knapp own goal gave the Midlanders the lead, but then the floodgates opened and in the next hour the Saints scored nine goals, with Martin Chivers grabbing four of them. The final score was 9–3, but the Saints had no reservations about the goalkeeper who let them in – they signed Wolves' goalkeeper Dave MacLaren.

When Southampton beat Ipswich Town 7–1 in the third round of the FA Cup on 7 January 1961, George O'Brien netted a hat-trick inside twenty eight minutes. In fact, in one spell, the Saints scored four goals in the space of seven minutes.

RAWLINGS, BILL

AFTER joining the Army in 1914, Bill Rawlings served in France with the Wessex Field Ambulance before joining Southampton in 1918 as an amateur. In 1918–19, the last season of wartime football, he scored sixteen goals in nine appearances to be the club's top scorer and in May 1919 was persuaded to turn professional.

Forging a good understanding with Arthur Dominy, he proved to be a prolific goal scorer and in the club's last season of Southern League football scored nineteen goals in thirty three games, including hat-tricks against Southend United (home 4–0) and Watford (home 5–1).

In 1920–21, the Saints' first season of league football, he was the club's leading scorer with eighteen goals, including four in a 5–0 home win over Merthyr Tydfil. When the Saints won the Third Division (South) Championship in 1921–22, Rawlings was in magnificent form, scoring thirty goals in thirty eight league games, including four in the matches against Northampton Town (home 8–0) and Millwall (home 4–2) and a hat-trick in the 6–0 defeat of Charlton Athletic.

Rawlings talents were recognised in 1922 when he won full international honours for England and played in the matches against Scotland and Wales.

In March 1928, after having scored 174 goals in 331 Football League and Cup games, he left The Dell to sign for Manchester United for £3,860. His stay at Old Trafford was short-lived and in November 1929 he joined Port Vale. He suffered a serious ankle injury at Vale Park which effectively ended his league career. In 1930 he moved on to New Milton and then Newport on the Isle of Wight, a club he helped win the Hampshire Senior Cup.

RECEIPTS

THE club's record receipts are £215,450 for the FA Cup third round match against Portsmouth at The Dell on 7 January 1996. A crowd of 15,236 saw the Saints win 3–0, with two goals from Jim Magilton and one from Neil Shipperley.

REEVES, DEREK

ONE of the greatest post-war centre-forwards in the club's history, Derek Reeves was discovered playing for Bournemouth Gasworks and signed for the Saints in December 1954.

He made his debut on 20 April 1955, scoring Southampton's goal in a 1–1 draw at Bournemouth. In 1955–56 he scored eighteen goals in thirty two games and the following season topped the club's scoring charts with nineteen goals in forty one games. In 1957–58 he again headed the scoring list with thirty one goals including hat-tricks against Queen's Park Rangers (home 5–0), Shrewsbury Town (away3–1) and Watford (home 5–0). He also scored four goals in the club's 6–1 FA Cup win at Walton and Hersham. He top scored again the following term with sixteen goals in thirty games, including four in a 6–1 win at Mansfield Town on the opening day of the season.

In 1959–60, when Southampton won the Third Division title, Reeves scored thirty nine league goals in forty six games, a Saints record that still stands. He scored four goals in a 5–1 home win over Swindon Town and hat-tricks against Southend United (away 4–2) and Mansfield Town (home 5–2). He also scored six goals in the FA Cup, four of them in a 5–1 win at Manchester City.

On 5 December 1960, he scored all five goals in a remarkable 5–4 League Cup fourth round victory over Leeds United. It was a tremendous performance by the Saints, down to ten men after having lost goalkeeper Reynolds.

Reeves went on to score 168 goals in 304 League and Cup games for the club before leaving The Dell in November 1962 to join Bournemouth for £8,000. He ended his league career at Dean Court, making thirty five appearances and scoring eight goals for the Cherries.

RELEGATION

SOUTHAMPTON have been relegated on only two occasions. Their first taste came in 1952–53 after being in the Second Division for thirty one years. The club had not really capitalised on the strong squad of players it had built up immediately after the war and although it finished fifteen points clear of bottom club Barnsley and enjoyed two eight goal thrillers against champions Sheffield United (home 4–4 and away 3–5) there was no reprieve.

The Saints' second experience of relegation was in 1973–74 after eight years in the First Division, yet if they had finished in twentieth place the previous season, they would have been safe. Defeat at Burnley on 22 April 1974 sealed their fate and yet five days later the Saints hammered seventh place Everton at Goodison Park 3–0.

ROBINSON, JACK

ALWAYS described as an agile and daring goalkeeper, Jack Robinson began his distinguished career with Derby St Neots and then Derby Midland before joining Lincoln City. He signed for Derby County during the 1890–91 season and with the Rams won his first full international cap when he played against Ireland at Nottingham in February 1897. Later that year he came into conflict with the football authorities when he joined New Brighton Tower, a club outside the FA's jurisdiction at the time.

He arrived at The Dell in 1898 and made his debut in the opening match of the 1898–99 season, a 4–1 home win over Brighton United. In the last game of that season the Saints travelled to Bristol City for a match that would determine the destiny of the Southern League Championship. Despite a badly sprained hand, Robinson refused to leave the field, helping the Saints to a 4–3 win and the title.

He was in trouble with the game's authorities for a second time when he tried to poach Steve Bloomer for Southampton when the England star was still at Derby.

During his five years at The Dell, Robinson won four Southern League Championship medals and appeared for England in five internationals. In May 1903 he joined Plymouth and followed this by playing for Millwall, Exeter, Plymouth (second spell), Exeter (second spell) and finally Stoke. When he arrived at the Victoria Ground he was forty three years old and became one of the oldest players to make his first appearance for the club. He emigrated to the USA and played until he was aged forty nine with Rochester before returning within a few years.

RODRIGUES, PETER

A FORMER Welsh Schoolboy and Youth international, Peter Rodrigues was introduced to league football by his home town club, Cardiff City. In December 1965 after he had made eighty five league appearances for the Ninian Park club, he signed for Leicester City for £45,000. In 1968–69 City were relegated to the Second Division but also reached the FA Cup Final, where they lost 1–0 to Manchester City.

Rodrigues, who by this time had been capped twenty three times at full level by Wales, was wanted by a number of top flight clubs but in October 1970 he joined Second Division Sheffield Wednesday for £50,000. At Hillsborough he took his tally of Welsh caps to forty but he could not prevent Wednesday from being relegated in 1974–75 and in the close season he joined Southampton.

He played his first game for the Saints in a 3–0 home win over West Bromwich Albion on the opening day of the 1975–76 season and missed just one game as the club finished fifth in the Second Division. His career had a fairy tale ending as he captained the Saints to victory over Manchester United in the FA Cup Final of 1976.

ROPER, DON

DON ROPER began his career with Southampton during the war years. He was originally a centre-forward but switched to the right-wing during 1943. By the time normal league football resumed, Roper had earned a reputation as a fast, two-footed winger and at the end of the 1946–47 season he joined Arsenal for £10,000, with Tom Rudkin going to The Dell in part exchange.

Roper had a memorable career at Highbury, helping the Gunners win the League Championship in his first season with the club. He won an FA Cup winners' medal in 1952 when he had to deputise at full-back for the injured Walley Barnes as Arsenal beat Newcastle United. The following season he scored five goals against Hibernian in a floodlit match at Highbury and represented England at B level. He went on to score ninety five goals in 321 League and Cup games before returning to The Dell for a second spell in January 1957.

He had two good seasons, netting eighteen goals in thirty eight games in 1957–58 before leaving league football at the end of the following season, having scored forty one goals in 127 first team games for the Saints. Roper later played for Weymouth and Dorchester and also played county cricket with Hampshire.

ROUGHTON, GEORGE

GEORGE ROUGHTON was an apprentice engineer, playing for amateur side Droylsden, when he signed for Huddersfield Town. He spent nine seasons with the Yorkshire club and in 1931 toured Canada with the FA and played for the Football League against the Irish League in 1934. In 1936 he returned to his native city to join Manchester United, where he was a key figure in the the club's side after promotion to the First Division.

In 1945 he became player/manager of Exeter City, retiring from the playing side at the end of the 1945–46 season to concentrate on management.

In March 1952 he was appointed manager of Southampton but in 1952–53, his first full season in charge, the club suffered relegation for the first time in their history. The Saints assumed that Roughton would lead them straight back to the Second Division but his health was failing and he resigned shortly after the start of the 1955–56 season.

ROWLEY, DICK

HAVING played his early football with Andover, Swindon and Corinthian Casuals, Dick Rowley arrived at The Dell in 1926, playing his first game for the Saints in the opening match of the 1926–27 season, a 3–1 defeat at Portsmouth.

That season saw the club enjoy a good run in the FA Cup with Rowley scoring five goals in their first three matches. He continued to find the net with great regularity and was inevitably attracting the attention of the First Division clubs. In 1929–30 he won the first of six international caps, four at The Dell when he played against Wales. That season he scored twenty five goals in twenty five games, including hat-tricks against Chelsea (home 4–2) and Nottingham Forest (away 5–0) before scoring four goals in a 5–2 win at Bradford City to become the first Southampton player to score four goals in an away league game. In January 1930, the Saints transferred Rowley, who had scored fifty seven goals in 113 League and Cup games, to Tottenham Hotspur for a fee of £3,750.

He went straight into the White Hart Lane club's side but as soon as Ted Harper was fit to resume he found himself confined to the reserves. With the arrival of George Hunt, Rowley now found himself third choice and after scoring eleven goals in twenty six games he and Ted Harper were transferred to Preston North End for a joint fee of £5,000. He wound up his career at Deepdale, scoring fourteen goals in fifty one league games.

RUDDOCK, NEIL

NEIL RUDDOCK came through the Millwall junior academy, first as an associated schoolboy and then as an apprentice, before turning professional in March 1986. A month later he joined Tottenham Hotspur without having made a single league appearance at The Den but at the end of the 1987–88 season, after making just league League and Cup appearances for the White Hart Lane club, he rejoined his former club which had just won promotion to the First Division. In eight months at The Den he failed to get a full ninety minutes play, although Millwall had paid £300,000 for him. He was on the move again, this time to Southampton in February 1989 for a fee of £250,000, to replace Kevin Moore at the heart of the Saints' defence. He soon established himself as a first team regular.

Neil Ruddock in action in defence.

In 1991–92 he was sent off twice and booked in every other game up to Christmas. He had played in 132 League and Cup games when, in another strange twist to his career, he returned to Tottenham Hotspur at the end of that season. He had played in forty seven games for Spurs when he informed Ossie Ardilles that he no longer wanted to play for the club. He was happy to sign for Liverpool when they met the London club's asking price of £2.5 million.The strong-tackling defender, who won an England cap against Nigeria in 1995, is still at Anfield, but has been unable to get a consistent run in the side despite having played in almost 150 games.

RUMBELOWS CUP

see Football League Cup.

RUNNERS–UP

THE Saints have been runners-up in a division of the Football League on four occasions: In 1920–21 in the Third Division South; in 1965–66 in the Second Division; in 1977–78, also in the Second Division; and 1983–84 in the First Division.

S

SCREEN SPORTS SUPER CUP

SOMETIMES known simply as the Super Cup. The trophy was contested just once during the 1985–86 season between the six teams which could have qualified for Europe. Southampton failed to win any of their four group matches, their results being: Liverpool (home 1–1, away 1–2) and Tottenham Hotspur (home 1–3, away 1–2).

SCRIVEN, BERT

GOALKEEPER Bert Scriven joined Southampton in 1930 after some outstanding performances for his local club, Totton. He made his debut for the Saints in a 2–1 defeat at Oldham Athletic on 8 September 1930. From then on, he was considered first-choice goalkeeper and in the next seven seasons he appeared in 233 League and Cup games, a total between the wars that was only beaten by Tommy Allen.

Scriven turned in a number of memorable performances but perhaps none more so than the FA Cup game against Birmingham in January 1935. The First Division side won 3–0 but not before he had made a series of miraculous saves.

He left The Dell in 1937 but continued to play non–League football with Salisbury.

SECOND DIVISION

SOUTHAMPTON have had three spells in the Second Division. After winning promotion in 1921–22, they had twenty four consecutive seasons of Second Division football before being relegated in 1952–53. During this spell their best position was third in seasons 1947–48 and 1948–49.

Promoted in 1959–60, the club's second spell in Division Two lasted six seasons before they won promotion to the First Division in 1965–66, finishing as runners-up, five points behind Manchester City.

The club's third and final spell in the Second Divison lasted just four seasons after relegation in 1973–74 as they ended the 1977–78 campaign as runners-up to Bolton Wanderers.

SEMI-FINALS

UP to the end of the 1997–98 season, Southampton had been involved in ten FA Cup semi-finals and two Football League Cup semi-finals.

SHEARER, ALAN

ALTHOUGH born in Newcastle, he signed for Southampton and made his Football League debut at Chelsea on 26 March 1988, as a substitute, a month before turning professional. In his first full league game, he caused a sensation, netting a hat-trick in a 4–2 win over Arsenal and becoming the youngest player to score three times in a First Division match.

In 1988–89 he was hampered by injuries and only played a handful of games but by the following season he was playing on a more regular basis. In 1990–91 he missed just four games as, with Le Tissier and Rod Wallace, he made the Saints into one of the most entertaining teams in the top flight. Remarkably, he only scored four goals in thirty six league games but netted eight in ten cup games.

In 1991–92, Saints' boss Ian Branfoot changed the club's style to an ultra-defensive one despite possessing, in Shearer and Le Tissier, two of the country's most exciting young forwards. Nevertheless,

Shearer finished as leading scorer with thirteen league goals, plus six in cup games, and missed only one match in the club's heavy programme of sixty matches.

Although he often found goals for the Saints hard to come by, he scored thirteen in eleven England Under–21 games before making his full international debut against France in February 1992, in which he scored England's first goal in a 2–0 win. He represented England in the European Championship Finals in Sweden but on his arrival home, signed for Blackburn Rovers for £3.6 million. Many felt the British record fee paid for the striker a little excessive but by Boxing Day 1992, Shearer proved it was a bargain, scoring twenty two goals in twenty five games. Unfortunately he was injured against Leeds and first needed a cartilage operation and then one to remove ligaments. After missing the start of the 1993–94 season he scored thirty four League and Cup goals and was by now the best striker in the country bar none.

On the opening day of the 1994–95 season, he missed a penalty against Southampton but it did not matter as he scored thurty seven League and Cup goals to be the country's top scorer and help Rovers win the Premier League title. In 1995–96 he repeated the feat, again scoring thirty seven goals. In doing so, he became the first player to reach 100 Premier League goals and also set a new record with five hat-tricks.

He had scored 128 goals in 162 League and Cup games when in July 1996, the England striker who had a superb Euro '96 tournament, joined Newcastle United for a world record £15 million. Despite being hindered by injury he duly lived up to expectations and was the Premier League's leading scorer.

Despite missing half the 1997–98 season through injury, he recovered to play for England in the World Cup in France.

SHELLEY, ALBERT

ALBERT SHELLEY signed for Southampton midway through the 1919–20 season after playing his early football with Romsey Comrades and Eastleigh Athletic in the Hampshire League.

Following an injury to Andrews in an FA Cup first round replay at West Ham, Shelley was given an extended run in the first team, only being on the losing side five times in the club's last eighteen games of the season. He went on to appear in 448 first team games for the club, to be an easy claimant of the Saints' appearance record at that time. The Romsey-born half-back was unlucky not to be capped by England but he did tour South Africa with the FA XI.

When his playing days were over in 1932, he became the club's youth team trainer and, three years later, first team trainer under the then Saints' manager, George Kay. When Kay moved to Liverpool in 1936, Shelley followed him and was still working behind the scenes at Anfield until he retired when Bob Paisley took over.

SHILTON, PETER

UNDOUBTEDLY one of the greatst goalkeepers of the modern era, Peter Shilton made his Football League debut for Leicester City as a sixteen year old and progressed to the point where he put manager Matt Gillies under pressure to either play him at the expense of Gordon Banks or let him go. In November 1974, after he had made 286 League appearances for the Filbert Street club, he joined Stoke City for £325,000, a world record fee for a goalkeeper.

However, following the Potters' relegation, he joined Nottingham Forest and in 1977–78, his first season at the City Ground, he kept twenty three clean sheets as Forest won the League Championship. At the City Ground, under Brian Clough, he also won two European Cup winners' medals, a League Cup winners' and runners up medal and a European Super Cup medal. In 1978 he was selected as the PFA Player of the Year.

He was unfortunate to have been around at the same time as Ray Clemence, who played sixty one times for England The number of caps he might have won, had he been unchallenged, might have spiralled towards the 200 mark. As it was, Shilton became England's most capped player with 125 international appearances to his name.

He left Forest in 1982 to join Southampton for £300,000. Making his debut in a 1–0 defeat at Coventry City in the opening game of the 1982–83 season, he was an ever-present the following season when he kept eighteen clean sheets as the Saints finished that campaign as First Division runners up to Liverpool.

Shilton played in 233 League and Cup games for the club before moving to Derby County in 1987. He later became player/manager of

Peter Shilton.

Plymouth Argyle before spells with Wimbledon, Bolton Wanderers, Coventry City, West Ham United and Leyton Orient.

No player in the history of the game has appeared in more Football League matches than 'Shilts'. He was deservedly awarded the MBE.

SIMOD CUP

THE Simod Cup replaced the Full Members' Cup for the 1987–88 season. The Saints first match in the newly named competition saw them lose 1–0 at Bradford City. In 1988–89, Stoke City were well beaten 3–0 but then in the next round, Crystal Palace won an exciting game at The Dell to put the Saints out.

SOUNESS, GRAEME

STARTING his career at Tottenham Hotspur, Soumes helped the White Hart Lane club win the FA Youth Cup in 1970 before progressing to the fringe of the first team. He had made just one appearance as a substitute for Alan Mullery in Keflavik in September 1971 when he grew impatient on the sidelines and returned home to Scotland.

Spurs allowed him to move to Middlesbrough and at the end of his first season the Ayresome Park club were promoted to the First Division. In January 1978 he was transferred to Liverpool where he matured into a world-class player. With the Anfield outfit he won almost every honour the game can offer before in July 1984 he turned his attention to Europe and joined Sampdoria of Italy. He returned to Britain as manager of Rangers and helped to bring honours galore to Ibrox Park, but in 1991 he returned to Liverpool as manager. After the shock of undergoing major heart surgery, he led the club to the FA Cup, the one trophy he failed to capture as a player before resigning in January 1994.

After managing Galatasaray, he took charge of Southampton in July 1996 and after making a number of low key signings brought in Eyal Berkovic, Egil Ostenstad and Ulrich van Gobbel. However, the Saints could only finish sixteenth in the Premier League and although they reached the League Cup quarter-finals, they were knocked out by Second Division Stockport County. At the end of a turbulent season, both Souness and Lawrie McMenemy quit the club.

SOUTHERN LEAGUE

WHEN the Southern League was formed in 1894 Southampton St Mary's, as the club were still known, had its application to join turned down. Fortunately for the Saints, the 2nd Scots Guards had to withdraw from the new competition before it started and St Mary's were subsequently offered their place.

Their first match was on 6 October 1894 when they beat Chatham 3–1 with Harry Offer scoring the club's first goal. The biggest win in their first season was 7–1 over Swindon at the Antelope and they ended the campaign in third place.

In 1896–97 the club left the Antelope Ground and took up temporaray residence at the Hampshire County Cricket Ground at Northlands Road. This move coincided with the Saints winning the Southern League Championship for the first time without losing a match. Millwall, who won the Championship in the first two years of the competition, provided the Saints' opposition for the final game of the season. Although they had already won the title they wanted to go through the season undefeated and had Joe Turner to thank for netting the equalising goal in a 1–1 draw.

Southampton retained the title the following season, finishing four points clear of Bristol City. Although not prolific scorers, their defence conceded only eighteen goals in twenty two matches, easily the best record in the division. The Saints managed to lose their first home game in the Southern League since January 1895 when they went down in their final home game of the season to Chatham by 1–0. It ended an unbeaten run spanning almost three and a half seasons.

In 1898–99 Southampton were champions for the third season running, just ahead of Bristol City. The championship hinged on the final game of the season against City at the St John's Ground, Bristol on 29 April. The Bristol club were unbeaten at home and led 2–0 at half-time. Saints looked out of it,, especially when goalkeeper Jack Robinson injured a hand. But they fought back and won a magnificent match 4–3 with goals from Wood (2), Chadwick and McLean to clinch the title by two points.

Champions for the last three seasons, the Saints were top of the table in February 1900 but their FA Cup run to the final interfered with the championship challenge. In 1900–01, the they won the Championship for the fourth time in five years, clinching the title with a 2–0 win over local rivals, Portsmouth, on 6 April 1901 with two goals from Alf Milward. Another vital game was the 1–1 draw with their closest rivals Bristol City in March when Bert Sharp scored Saints' goal. Surprisingly, there was a decline in attendances at The Dell, which was blamed on admission prices being doubled for the bigger games. The club lost £740 on the year.

In 1901–02, the Saints made their record win of 11–0 against Northampton Town, when Albert Brown scored seven times. This record still stands today.

They began the following season in great style, beating Brentford 6–0 with new signing, Jack Fraser, scoring a hat-trick. The Saints lost just two games, both to Tottenham, but won the Championship for a fifth time, ending the season three points ahead of Reading. They won it for a sixth time in 1903–04 – a most satisfying achievement as the Saints had become the side everyone wanted to beat. The following season was a disappointing one by the Saints' standards, the many comings and goings on the transfer market unsettling the side. They lost their last four home games which was unheard of in those days and were beaten 6–1 at champions Bristol Rovers on 11 March 1905.

In 1905–06, the club finished runners up to Fulham but were affected by the Southern League's imposition of a wage limit which hit the bigger clubs.

The following season, the Saints finished only eleventh. After three seasons of mid-table placings they plunged to seventeenth, their worst position since joining the Southern League in 1894.

In the seasons leading up to the First World War, Southampton hovered near the foot of the table and only when the competition resumed after the hostilities did they begin to show any form reminiscent of the early years in the Southern League. In what was to be the last season in that league, the club finished in eighth place.

SPONSORS

SOUTHAMPTON'S present sponsors are Sanderson's Electronics. The club's previous sponsors include Draper Tools, Dimplex and Rank Xerox.

STEELE, JIM

EDINBURGH-born defender Jim Steele arrived at The Dell from Dundee in January 1972 for a fee of £65,000 and with a bad disciplinary record. His first match for the Saints saw Nottingham Forest beaten 4–1 but the rest of the season was an uphill struggle against relegation.

By 1972–73 Steele had adjusted well to English football and his maturity had much to do with the club's improved defensive record which saw them end the season in thirteenth place.

Although he could play full-back, the predominantly left-sided Steele was much happier in the middle of defence and it was when wearing the Number

Six shirt that he had his best games.

When the Saints won the FA Cup in 1976, Steele was voted Man of the Match in the final against Manchester United but after playing in 188 League and Cup games, the popular Scot left league football prematurely to play for Washington Diplomats in the NASL.

STOKES, BOBBY

ONE of the most popular players ever to wear the red and white stripes of Southampton, Bobby Stokes scored two goals on his Saints debut in a 5–1 home win over Burnley in April 1969. He also scored in his next game at The Dell as Manchester City were beaten 3–0. However, it was 1971–72 before he won a regular place in the Southampton line up, playing in all but the last game of the season.

Although on the small side for a striker, Stokes scored the most important goal in the club's history, when on 1 May 1976 he latched on to Jim McCalliog's perfect through ball and slotted it past Alex Stepney in the Manchester United goal to give the Saints a 1–0 victory in the FA Cup Final.

He had scored fifty two goals in 244 League and Cup games when in the summer of 1977 he left The Dell to join his home team, Portsmouth. Also at this time, he linked up with former Southampton players Eric Martin and Jim Steele at Washington Diplomats in the NASL. When he returned to these shores he joined Cheltenham Town then managed by Terry Paine.

Sadly, Bobby died in May 1995 at the tragically young age of forty four.

SUBSTITUTES

THE first Southampton substitute was Ken Wimshurst who came on for injured goalkeeper John Hollowbread in a 1–0 home win over Coventry City on 8 September 1965.

The club had to wait until 29 April 1967 for the first goalscoring substitute – Martin Chivers scoring in a 3–1 defeat at Newcastle United. The greatest number of substitutes used in a single season by Southampton under the single substitute rule was twenty six in 1974–75 but after 1986–87 two substitutes were allowed and in 1994–95, fifty two were used.

The greatest number of substitute appearances in the Football League for Southampton has been made by Nicky Banger who came on in thirty seven league games with four more in cup ties. It was Banger who rewrote the Southampton records on substitutes when, in 1992–93, he made an extraordinary sixteen league appearances in the substitute's shirt.

SUSTAINED SCORING

RON DAVIES holds the club record for consecutive scoring when he was on target in ten consecutive league games. His first came in the 1–0 win at Aston Villa on 5 September 1966 and ended with two goals in the 3–2 home win over Stoke City on 5 November 1966. Despite playing in a struggling team, he was the First Division's leading scorer with thirty seven goals.

SWIFT, GEORGE

SOUTHAMPTON'S first secretary/manager appeared in the Football Alliance for Crewe and in the FA Cup Final of 1893 for Wolverhampton Wanderers. Afterwards he played for Loughborough and was the club's only player to win a senior representative honour when he appeared for the Football League against the Irish League in 1895. A year later he joined Leicester Fosse, where he became captain and was ever-present in four of his six seasons with the club.

After retiring from the playing side he became trainer at Leeds City, although he did have one game on the left wing in an emergency against Chelsea in 1906. He took up his first managerial position with Chesterfield in 1907 but the Derbyshire club had to seek re–election in his first two seasons in charge and was voted out of the league in 1909.

Appointed at The Dell in April 1911, Swift spent the first six weeks searching for new players and spent more than £1,200 on recruits. However, they all proved failures and in 1911–12 after the club finished sixteenth in the Southern League, Swift resigned.

SYDENHAM, JOHN

A MEMBER of the Southampton side which had a good run in the FA Youth Cup of 1956–57, he made his first team debut in the final game of that season, starring in a 3–0 home win over Newport County when his bursts of speed and pin–point crosses led to two of the club's goals.

An England Youth international, he went on to win two caps at Under–23 level, the first against France in 1959. In 1959–60 he won a Third Division Championship winners' medal. Missing just one game, he created a host of chances for Reeves and O'Brien who scored sixty two league goals between them.

At the end of that season, Sydenham was called up for National Service which not only interrupted his progress but also unsettled him. For a time he wanted to leave The Dell, but thankfully had second thoughts and played an important role in the club winning promotion to the First Division in 1965–66.

He was never a prolific goalscorer, netting thirty nine goals in 395 League and Cup games, but he was quite content to make chances for others. Probably his finest game in Southampton colours came on 16 August 1969 when he provided a seemingly never-ending stream of crosses for Ron Davies to score all four goals in a 4–1 win for the Saints against Manchester United at Old Trafford.

In March 1970 he was allowed to leave The Dell and joined Aldershot for which he made fifty eight league appearances. He then had a spell in management on the Isle of Wight before emigrating to Perth in Australia where he coached a local side.

SYMMETRICAL RECORD

SOUTHAMPTON finished the 1922–23 season with a symmetrical record in the Second Division. They had forty two points from forty two matches; fourteen wins, fourteen draws and fourteen defeats; forty goals for and forty goals against.

T

TELEVISION

SOUTHAMPTON'S first appearance on BBC's *Match of the Day* was on 29 October 1966 when they beat Leeds United 1–0 at Elland Road in front of a 32,232 crowd, with Ron Davies the Saints' goal scorer.

On 16 March 1984 Liverpool visited The Dell for the first match to be televised live from the ground under a new agreement between the Football League and the television companies. A nationwide audience, plus a crowd of 19,698 inside The Dell, saw two superb goals from Danny Wallace earn Saints a 2–0 win.

TENNANT–CALEDONIAN CUP

ALL the games in this competition were played at Ibrox Park, Glasgow and in 1976–77, the first time Southampton participated, they won the trophy. After drawing 1–1 with Manchester City, the game went to a penalty shoot out but after each player had scored to make it 11–11, the Saints went through on the toss of a coin. In the final, goals from Channon and Peach gave the club a 2–1 win over Glasgow Rangers.

The following season, Southampton lost 3–1 to Glasgow Rangers but then beat St Mirren 2–1 in a third place play-off match. In 1977–78, Saints beat West Bromwich Albion 4–1 on penalties after the match had ended all square at 1–1 but then lost 4–1 in the final to Glasgow Rangers with Ted MacDougall netting for the Saints.

TEXACO CUP

THIS predecessor of the Anglo-Scottish Cup was launched in 1970–71 for English, Irish and Scottish club sides not involved in European competitions. The Saints only entered during the 1974–75 season and reached the final. Unbeaten in their group matches – Luton Town (away 1–1), Orient home 2–1) and West Ham United (home 2–0) – the club entered the two legged knockout stages. After a 3–1 win at Ibrox Park against

Glasgow Rangers in which Peter Osgood scored two goals, the Saints won 2–0 at The Dell to win 5–1 on aggregate. Oldham Athletic provided the semi-final opposition but two goals from Mick Channon helped Saints to a 3–1 win at Boundary Park. Channon was on the score sheet again in the second leg which Southampton won 2–1 to reach the final 5–2 on aggregate. Against Newcastle United in the final a Mick Channon goal gave the Saints a first leg win at The Dell but at St James' Park they lost 3–0 after extra time and so the Cup went to the Magpies.

THIRD DIVISION

SOUTHAMPTON have had two spells in the Third Division. Their first lasted just two seasons. They entered the Football League in 1920–21 andts finished runners up to Crystal Palace but then won the Third Division (South) Championship in 1921–22 on goal difference from Plymouth Argyle. The club then had twenty four seasons of Second Division football before relegation in 1952–53 led to their second spell in Division Three. This time the Saints spent seven seasons in the Third Division before winning the title in 1959–60, finishing two points ahead of Norwich City.

TITMUSS, FRED

AFTER playing his early football for his home club, Hitchin, full-back Fred Titmuss joined the army. It was while he was playing for the various army teams that he was spotted by Saints' trainer Bert Lee, who persuaded him to join Southampton.

A fine exponent of the sliding tackle, he made his Saints' debut in the club's first game after the First World War, a 1–1 home draw against Exeter City. Titmuss and Tom Parker developed a fine understanding and were arguably the best pair of full-backs in the country and both were capped by England – Titmuss against Wales in 1922 and 1923 while a Second Division player.

Surprisingly in the spring of 1926, the directors sold Titmuss to Plymouth Argyle for £1,750, after the full-back had appeared in 237 first team games for the club. He then went on to spend six successful seasons at Home Park before leaving to play part time for St Austell.

TOURS

AT the end of the 1900–01 season, the Saints embarked on their first foreign tour, taking in Belgium, Austria and Hungary. The club won all six matches, scoring forty four goals and conceding just three.

After winning the Southern League Championship in 1902–03, the Saints toured the same three countries and Denmark, winning all their games, two of them by scorelines of 15–0. At the end of the following season, Southampton became the first English team to tour Argentina. They impressed the Argentinians so much that the government ordered that the game be taught to all army regiments. The Saints were also the first English League club to tour Brazil when they did so in the summer of 1948.

TOWNSEND, ANDY

AFTER starting his career with Welling United in the Southern League, he joined Weymouth, thus stepping up one grade to what was then the Gola League. After only half a season with the Dorset club, his performances attracted the attention of Southampton who signed him in January 1985 for £35,000.

He did not make an immediate impact in the First Division and had to wait until the end of the season before making his debut at left-back in a 2–0 home win over Aston Villa. In 1985–86 he played twenty seven games, alternating between left-back and midfield but missed the first half of the following season after breaking a leg in a pre-season friendly against his old club Weymouth.

Andy Townsend.

In 1987–88 he established himself

as a commanding midfield player but in the summer of 1988 he was rather surprisingly sold to Norwich City. He helped the Canaries to their highest ever League position of fourth in the First Division and to the semi-finals of the FA Cup. He also won international recognition with the Republic of Ireland, making his debut against France in February 1989. After one more season at Carrow Road he was transferred to Chelsea for £1.2 million but after three years in which he confirmed his reputation as one of the leading midfield operators in the top flight, he joined Aston Villa for £2 million.

A tremendous competitor, he made 131 League appearances for Villa before he signed for Middlesbrough in 1997.

TRANSFERS

THE club's record transfer fee received is £7million from Blackburn Rovers for the services of Kevin Davies in the summer of 1998. Southampton's record transfer fee paid is £1.4 million to Galatasaray for Ulrich van Gobbel in October 1996.

TRAYNOR, TOMMY

FULL-BACK Tommy Traynor began his footballing career with his home team, Dundalk, and had represented the Republic of Ireland at amateur level when he joined Southampton in the summer of 1952.

He made his debut in a 3–0 defeat at Brentford on 11 October 1952 and soon gained a regular place in the Saints' first team. At The Dell he won eight full caps, the first against Luxembourg in 1954 and the last against Spain ten years later.

An ever-present in 1954–55 when the Saints finished third in Division Three (South) he won a Third Division Championship medal in 1959–60 when his influence and presence both on and off the field helped the club finish two points ahead of Norwich City. During the 1963–64 season he passed Albert Shelley's league appearance record for the club. Feared by the opposition, this strong-tackling defender went on to appear in 480 League and Cup games for the Saints, playing his last game in a 5–2 home win over Preston North End on 27 November 1965, the season in which the club gained promotion to the First Division.

TURNER, JOE

OUTSIDE-LEFT Joe Turner joined the Saints from Dresden United in 1895 and made his first team debut at Millwall in the opening game of the 1895–96 season.

In 1896–97 he was the club's second highest scorer in the Southern League and scored in each of the five rounds of the FA Cup that the club were involved in. The following season he was joint top scorer and netted his first hat-trick for the club in a 4–1 home win over New Brompton as the Saints ended the season as League Champions. However, at the end of that campaign, he was allowed to join Stoke and a year later moved to Everton before rejoining Southampton for a second spell in 1901.

He appeared for the Saints in the FA Cup Final of 1902 and helped them win the Southern League Championship again in 1902–03 when his fourteen goals included another hat-trick in a 6–0 win over West Ham United on the final day of the season.

He had scored fifty six goals in 124 games when in 1904, he joined New Brompton.

U

UEFA CUP

SOUTHAMPTON'S first opponents in the newly named UEFA Cup, formerly the Fairs Cup, were Athletico Bilbao. Goals from Channon and Jenkins gave the Saints a 2–1 home win but despite a determined effort in Spain, Bilbao won 2–0 to take the tie 3–2 on aggregate.

In 1981–82 Southampton beat Limerick 4–1 on aggregate but then went out in the next round to Sporting Lisbon. The Saints lost the home leg 4–2 before playing out a goal-less draw in Portugal. The following season the Saints went out of the competition on the away goals rule. Facing Norrkoping, Southampton drew the home leg 2–2 and despite a number of chances in the second leg, the game ended without a goal being scored and the Saints were out.

Southampton last played in the UEFA Cup in 1984–85 but after being held to a 0–0 draw at The Dell by Hamburg lost in Germany 2–0 to go out at the first hurdle.

The club did qualify for the 1985–86 UEFA Cup but the Football League clubs were banned because of the tragedy at the previous season's European Cup Final between Liverpool and Juventus.

UNDEFEATED

SOUTHAMPTON were undefeated at home throughout just one Football League season, 1921–22, when they won the Third Division (South) Championship. Their best and longest undefeated sequence in the Football League is of nineteen matches between 5 September 1921 and 14 January 1922. Southampton's longest run of undefeated Football League matches at The Dell is thirty one between 22 January 1921 and 28 August 1922.

UTILITY PLAYERS

A UTILITY player is one of those particularly gifted footballers who can play in a number of different positions. Two of the club's earliest utility players were Sam Meston and Jack Robertson. Meston, who played in six different positions, won a record six Southern League Championship medals. Robertson, primarily a defender, turned out in seven different positions for the club.

After the mid-1960s players were encouraged to become more adaptable and to see their roles as less stereotyped. At the same time, however, much less attention came to be paid to the implication of wearing a certain numbered shirt and accordingly, some of the more versatile players like Graham Baker and Nick Holmes came to wear almost all the different numbered shirts at some stage or another, although this did not necessarily indicate a vast variety of positions.

V W

VICTORIES IN A SEASON – HIGHEST

IN the 1959–60 season, the Saints won twenty six of their forty six league fixtures to win the Third Division championship with sixty one points, the highest in the club's history under the old two points for a win system.

VICTORIES IN A SEASON – LOWEST

SOUTHAMPTON'S poorest performance was in 1969–70 when they won only six matches out of their forty two games to finish nineteenth in the First Division.

WALKER, DAVID

WING-HALF David Walker was serving his apprentice ship as an engineer when he joined Burnley as an amateur in the summer of 1958. He signed professional forms a year later and went on to make forty first team appearances over the next two seasons before joining Southampton in May 1965 for £20,000.

He made his debut in a 3–0 win at Derby County on the opening day of the 1965–66 season and was a regular in the Saints side as they went on to win promotion to Division One for the first time as runners up to Manchester City. Over the next nine seasons, Walker played in 224 League and Cup games in a Southampton defence that had gained something of a reputation for being uncompromising.

In February 1974 he moved out to South Africa to play and coach at Capetown City, later returning to live in Southampton where he built up a successful antiques business.

WALLACE, DANNY

AT sixteen years 313 days old Danny Wallace became Southampton's youngest player when he made his Football League debut while still an apprentice in a 1–1 draw at Manchester United on 29 November 1980.

Elder brother of twins Ray and Rod, he won a regular place in the team on the left-wing from October 1982 and finished the season as top scorer with twelve league goals. In 1983–84 he missed only one game as the club achieved their highest placing, second, only three points behind champions Liverpool.

Wallace was the club's first-choice left-winger for the next five seasons and although he won fourteen England Under–21 caps between 1982 and 1985, he made only one full international appearance in England's first international against Egypt in Cairo in January 1986. He scored once in a 4–0 victory but was never selected again.

By 1988–89, his last full season at The Dell, he was overshadowed by the exploits of younger brother Rod on the right wing and in September 1989 after scoring seventy four goals in 311 League and Cup games he moved to Manchester United for £1.2million.

It was not a happy move for the Greenwich-born winger, for even though he won an FA Cup medal when United beat Crystal Palace, he could not win a regular place in the Reds' line up. In October 1993 he joined Birmingham City for £250,000 but after only sixteen league games for the St Andrews' club he moved to Wycombe Wanderers where he ended his career.

WALLACE, ROD

BROTHER of Danny, he made his Football League debut while still a trainee when coming on as a substitute at Newcastle United in September 1987. He celebrated his new professional status with a goal in his second full appearance – a late equaliser against Liverpool at Anfield.

In his first full season, 1988–89, he was ever-present and top scorer with twelve league goals. He enjoyed another superb season in 1989–90 with remarkably fourteen of his eighteen goals being scored in braces. The following season was more of a struggle for the team but he still achieved fourteen league goals, second only to Le Tissier. It was inevitable perhaps but sad that he should leave The Dell for a bigger club and in the summer of 1991 after scoring fifty three goals in 157 games, he joined Leeds United with twin brother Ray.

He soon established himself as a crowd favourite at Elland Road and in his first season helped the club win the League Championship. In

1992–93 he was rewarded with a call to the England squad for the friendly in Spain but unfortunately he received an injury at Old Trafford and was put out of action for seven weeks, thus losing the opportunity.

In 1995–96 he twice turned down the opportunity of a return to Southampton after a fee had been agreed between the two clubs. Still one of the most skilful and direct players in the Premier League, he has played in more than 200 games for the Yorkshire side.

WARTIME FOOTBALL

IN spite of the outbreak of war in 1914, the various football leagues embarked upon their planned programme of matches for the ensuing season and these were completed on schedule at the end of April the following year. The season saw the club finish sixth in the Southern League. In 1915–16 the Saints played friendly matches mainly against Southern League clubs and in the second half of the season, the South Western Combination was formed.

The Saints did well, finishing runners up to Portsmouth. For the 1916–17 season the club joined the London Combination but at the end of the campaign, in which the Saints finished ninth, the London clubs proposed to expel Southampton, Portsmouth, Luton and Watford on the grounds that as the war went on, railway travel was becoming increasingly difficult. The Saints took part in the South Hants War League as they did in 1918–19, finishing fourth on each occasion. They supplemented their league fixtures with a series of friendly matches but more often than not, the regular Southampton players appeared for the opposition.

In contrast to the events of 1914, once war was declared on 3 September 1939, the Football League programme of 1939–40 was immediately suspended and the government banned any major sporting events, so that for a short while there was no football of any description.

Organised football returned in late October and the Saints were placed in the Football League South B. Sadly they finished bottom of the ten clubs, suffering their heaviest defeat 9–4 at Brighton. An additional competition was played at the end of the season, against nearly all different opposition, the Saints improving to finish eighth.

In 1940–41, the first full season of wartime football, the club had to endure a number of tedious journeys after The Dell was bombed in

November 1940, and an 18ft wide crater in one of the penalty areas made the ground unplayable for the rest of the season.

In a league table calculated on goal average, Southampton finished thirty first out of thirty three clubs. In 1941–42 the London clubs and Portsmouth joined the London competition and so Southampton were left to arrange fixtures when they could, although they managed ten League South fixtures. After a two year absence, the London clubs returned and in a much improved season, the Saints finished fifth in the League South, beating Luton Town 11–0 with Alf Whittingham, a guest player scoring eight of the goals.

The club had a disappointing season in 1943–44 and suffered their worst defeat, losing 10–1 to an Aldershot side packed with guest players. The Saints did much better the following season, finishing fifth in the League South after beating Watford 9–0 in the opening match of the season. In 1945–46 the old programme of forty two matches was reintroduced in preparation for the resumption of league football the following season. In a season of ups and downs, the club finished sixteenth in the League South but did beat Chelsea 7–0 with Doug McGibbon scoring a double hat-trick.

WATSON, DAVE

DAVE WATSON played for Stapleford Old Boys before joining Notts County and was a centre-forward first and foremost. He moved on to Rotherham United, where he was switched to centre-half by Millmoor boss, Tommy Docherty. He then moved on for big money transfers to Sunderland, Manchester City and Werder Bremen before joining Southampton in October 1979 for a fee of £200,000.

Having won an FA Cup winners' medal in 1973 at Sunderland and a League Cup winners' medal in 1976 at Manchester City, he made his Saints' debut in a 4–0 defeat at West Bromwich Albion. Despite this setback he fitted in well, bringing a vast experience to the heart of the Southampton defence. He stayed at The Dell for two and a half seasons, playing in eighty one League and Cup games before joining Stoke City for £50,000.

He enjoyed one and a half good seasons at the Victoria Ground, before moving to play for Vancouver Whitecaps in the NASL. On his return he linked up with Derby County, later playing for Fort Lauderdale Sun, Notts County and Kettering Town.

WAYMAN, CHARLIE

CHARLIE WAYMAN was born in Bishop Auckland and started his working life in the coal mines. After playing for Chilton Colliery and Spennymoor United, he joined Newcastle United for whom he proved to be a prolific goal scorer in the War Leagues.

When league football was resumed in 1946 Wayman was a regular in the Magpies' forward line and in that season topped the Second Division scoring charts with thirty goals as well as netting a hat-trick to knock Southampton out of the FA Cup.

Surprisingly, he was allowed to leave St James' Park and in October 1947, Saints' manager Bill Dodgin paid £10,000 to bring Wayman to The Dell. Settling in immediately, he scored seventeen goals in twenty seven league games as the Saints ended the season in third place in Division Two. The following season he scored five goals in a 6–0 home win over Leicester City, creating a club record that still stands today.

On 2 April 1949, the Saints travelled to White Hart Lane to meet fellow promotion rivals Tottenham Hotspur. A crowd of 69,265 saw them suffer a massive blow when Wayman tore a thigh muscle and had to go out on to the wing where he became a virtual passenger. The Saints still pressed forward and after Bates had hit the woodwork, he slipped a through ball to Wayman who momentarily forgot his pain. His first shot was parried by Ditchburn but the little striker followed up to score the only goal of the game with his injured right leg.

The Saints were now eight points clear of Fulham and West Bromwich Albion with seven games to play. Wayman's injury worsened and he did not play again that season. Without him, the Saints only picked up four of a possible fourteen points and finished the season in third place.

In 1949–50 Wayman scored twenty four goals in thirty six league games, including a hat-trick in a 5–0 home win over Hull City, but the Saints ended the season on fifty two points, as did both Sheffield clubs. Tottenham Hotspur were the champions and Sheffield Wednesday were promoted with them on goal average.

Wayman's wife had never really settled in the south and after scoring eighty one goals in 107 League and Cup games he moved to Preston North End. In his first season with the Deepdale club he scored four goals in the first half against Queen's Park Rangers at Loftus Road on Christmas Day and ended the campaign with twenty seven goals. His flair for snatching scintillating goals also earned him a memorable hat-trick against Arsenal at Highbury. During North End's FA Cup run of 1954, the courageous Wayman scored in every round including the final against West Bromwich Albion.

He later played for Middlebrough and Darlington and having scored 254 goals in 382 games for his five clubs, he hung up his boots.

WILKINS, LEN

DISCOVERED by Southampton when playing on the Common, Len Wilkins made his debut for the Saints as a half-back in a 6–0 home win over Leicester City in October 1948 in a match in which Charlie Wayman scored five goals. He played in all the remaining twenty nine games that season as the Saints finished third in the Second Division.

Wilkins was one of Southampton's great unsung heroes and in 1954–55 when the club finished third in Division Three (South) he was an ever-present after being tried at centre-half with great success.

In 1957–58, his last season at The Dell, he was made team captain and when he made the last of his 274 League and Cup appearances for the Saints, this most popular of players was given a great ovation.

WILLIAMS, STEVE

ONE of the best midfield players Southampton ever produced, Steve Williams turned professional in September 1975 and went straight into the Saints' first team without first appearing for the club's reserve side. He made his debut in a 1–0 win at Portsmouth on 6 April 1976 and in the next nine seasons went on to play in 335 League and Cup games.

He helped the club to the 1979 League Cup Final and to First Division runners up position in 1983–84. He also won six England caps, four B caps and fourteen Under–21 caps. He would have won many more at full international level had it not been for his temperament which let him

Steve Williams.

down on many occasions. Lawrie McMenemy managed to curb most of Williams' aggression and even made him team captain, but in December 1984, he left The Dell to join Arsenal, the team he had supported as a boy, for £550,000.

His early days at Highbury were hampered by injuries but in 1986–87 he helped the Gunners to the Littlewoods Cup victory against Liverpool. Unfortunately a rift developed between Williams and Arsenal manager George Graham and in July 1988 he was transferred to Luton Town for £300,000. He spent two seasons at Kenilworth Road before finishing his career with his ex-Saints team-mate, Alan Ball, at Exeter City.

WILLIAMS, STUART

STUART WILLIAMS began his footballing career as an amateur with his home team, Wrexham, making his league debut for the Racecourse Ground club against Rochdale in April 1949.

He joined West Bromwich Albion in February 1951 and three years later won the first of forty three Welsh caps when he played against Austria. In eleven seasons at The Hawthorns, Williams played in 226 league games, but in September 1962 at the age of thirty two, he signed for Southampton.

He made his debut for the Saints in a 2–1 home win over Chelsea and later in that 1962–63 season, scored his first goal for the club in a 4–2 home win over local rivals Portsmouth. He went on to appear in 167 League and Cup games for the club before returning to West Bromwich Albion as coach in the summer of 1966. In September 1971 he went back to The Dell as assistant manager to Ted Bates.

WIMSHURST, KEN

HALF-BACK Ken Wimshurst began his career with Newcastle United before moving to Gateshead, where he made his league debut. Wolverhampton Wanderers signed him but he failed to make the first team at Molineux and in the summer of 1961 he joined Southampton for a fee of £1,500.

Wimshurst had been recommended by scout, Bill Rochford, and the club had cause to thank him, for the South Shields-born wing-half went on to give Saints six seasons good service. He made his debut in a 5–1 home win over Swansea Town on 2 September 1961 and went on to play in 171 League and Cup games. Perhaps his best spell came in the club's FA Cup run of 1962–63 when he played in all seven games and scored in the victories over York City and Nottingham Forest.

A clever passer of the ball, he left The Dell in October 1967 to join Bristol City for £12,000. He went on to play in 149 league games for the Robins before working behind the scenes at Ashton Gate. He later had a stint coaching in Egypt.

WOOD, HARRY

HARRY WOOD began his career with his home club, Walsall Town Swifts, before joining Wolverhampton Wanderers in 1887. He was soon capped twice by England at full international level and in 1893 won an FA Cup winners' medal.

In 1898, Saints' trainer Dawson was visiting relatives in the Birmingham area and after hearing that Wood was unsettled at Molineux, decided to investigate the matter further. After making inquiries in a local pub, Wood was contacted and signed there and then for the Saints.

Nicknamed 'The Wolf', he made his debut for Southampton in the opening game of the 1898–99 season in a 4–1 home win over Brighton United. The club went on to win the Southern League Championship and Wood was the leading scorer with sixteen goals including a hat-trick in the 6–0 home win over Sheppey United.

He was made captain and led the club through one of the most successful period in its history as it reached the FA Cup Final in 1900 and 1902 and won the Southern League Championship in seasons 1900–01, 1902–03 and 1903–04.

In 1905 after scoring sixty two goals in 158 games for the Saints, he hung up his boots to become Portsmouth's trainer, a position he held for five years.

WOODHOUSE, SID

SIGNED from Bury in the summer of 1924, Sid Woodhouse made his debut at inside-forward in the opening game of the 1924–25 season, a goal-less home draw against Oldham Athletic. By the start of the following season he had been switched to half-back, a position he was to excel in over the next twelve seasons. He only missing a handful of games due to injury and appeared in 365 League and Cup games for the Saints, a figure that put him second only to Albert Shelley at the time. He left The Dell in 1936 to end his career with non-League Basingstoke.

WORST START

THE club's worst start to a season was in 1996–97 when it took eight games to record their first victory. It had taken a similar length of time to win their first match in 1937–38 and 1976–77. In 1996–97 only two of their first seven matches were drawn with five being lost. The run ended with a 4–0 success over Middlesbrough that saw them embark on a five match unbeaten run before losing five straight matches. The Saints ended the season in sixteenth place in the Premiership.

WRIGHT, MARK

AFTER beginning his league career with Oxford United, he was used as a makeweight in a complicated deal which took him and Keith Cassells to Southampton in exchange for Trevor Hebberd and George Lawrence.

While Cassells never made the grade at The Dell, Wright became a fixture in central defence from the start of the 1982–83 season after making his Saints debut as a forward in a 3–1 win at Leeds United in April 1982.

After four appearances for the England Under–21 side, he graduated to the national team, winning the first of what is now forty five caps against Wales at Wrexham in May 1984. He became an England regular the following season but was unavailable for the 1986

World Cup Finals in Mexico due to a broken leg suffered in the FA Cup semi-final against Liverpool.

Apart from a well publicised fracas with Lawrie McMenemy, Wright had five good years at The Dell, playing in 212 League and Cup games. He joined Peter Shilton in moving to Derby County as part of Robert Maxwell's drive to establish the Rams as a First Division force.

One of the heroes of England's 1990 World Cup campaign, he left the Baseball Ground in the summer of 1991, signing for Liverpool for a fee of £2.2million. He captained the Anfield club to FA Cup success in 1992 when they beat Sunderland 2–0 and although he has appeared in almost 200 League and Cup games for the Reds, for much of his time on Merseyside he has been hampered by injuries.

X

X

IN football X traditionally stands for a draw. The club record for the number of draws in a season is eighteen, which was achieved in seasons 1924–25 when the Saints finished seventh in Division Two; 1972–73, thirteenth in Division One; and 1994–95, tenth in the Premier League.

XMAS DAY

THERE was a time when football matches were regularly played on Christmas Day but in recent years the game's authorities have dropped the fixture from their calendar.

Southampton first played on Christmas Day in 1902 when goals from Lee and Turner gave them a 2–1 win at West Ham United in a Southern League fixture. Their first Football League game to be played on Christmas Day was in the initial season when a Jimmy Moore goal gave them a 1–1 draw at Luton Town.

On Christmas Day 1934, a Laurie Fishlock goal gave the Saints a 1–0 win against Swansea Town at Vetch Field and so ended a sequence of thirty four matches without an away win that went back to April 1932.

One of the most unusual incidents to occur in the club's Christmas Day fixtures was during the wartime games. In 1941, the Saints' opponents at The Dell were Bristol City. They left Ashton Gate in three cars, the last two carrying two players and the kit. This vehicle arrived first but as time for the kick off approached, there was no sign of the other two cars

Saints' boss Tom Parker offered City five reserve players plus the club's trainer but even then they were only up to eight men, so three spectators got changed to make up the side. The game kicked off an hour late but after twenty minutes, the other nine Bristol players arrived in one car, the other having broken down. The Saints eventually won 5–2 with Howard scoring four of the goals. At half time City were three goals down and had one of their spectator reserves injured. They tried to replace him with one of their own latecomers, Ernie Brinton. He changed into a muddy kit and applied mud to his face, hair and knees to look as if he had been playing all the match. As he took a throw-in during the early stages of the second half, an eagle-eyed linesman spotted him and he was immediately sent back to the dressing room.

The first game to be played on Christmas Day after the hostilities saw the Saints play out an exciting 4–4 draw at Barnsley with Tom Lewis netting two of the goals.

The last time Southampton played on Christmas Day was 1958 when they lost 4–2 at Newport County.

Y Z

YOUNGEST PLAYER

THE youngest player to appear in a first class fixture for Southampton is Danny Wallace, who played in the First Division match against Manchester United (away 1–1) on 29 November 1980 when he was sixteen years 313 days old.

ZENITH

FEW fans will argue over which moment has been the finest in the club's history. Bobby Stokes scored the most important goal in the Saints' history on 1 May 1976 to bring the FA Cup to Second Division Southampton for the first time after a 1–0 win over First Division Manchester United.

ZENITH DATA SYSTEMS CUP

THE Zenith Data Systems Cup replaced the Simod Cup for the 1990–91 season. The club's first match in this competition saw them beat Queen's Park Rangers 4–0, but then lose 2–1 at Norwich City in the Southern Area quarter–final.

In 1991–92 the Saints reached the final, beating Bristol City (2–1 away); Plymouth Argyle (1–0 away); West Ham United (2–1 home); and Chelsea (2–0 home). At Wembley, Southampton lost 3–2 to Nottingham Forest after extra time with Le Tissier and Moore netting for the Saints.

ACKNOWLEDGEMENTS

The author wishes to thank the following for their invaluable assistance in producing this book:
Southampton Football Club, the staff of the Central Reference Library, Southampton and Steve Benz for his continued support in this A-Z series.

PICTURE CREDITS

Illustrations were kindly supplied by the *Lancashire Evening Post,* the *Liverpool Daily Post and Echo,* the *Stockport Express Advertiser,* and the *Manchester Evening News.*
The cigarette cards were supplied by Peter Stafford.A number of illustrations are from the author's own collection.

FRONT COVER PICTURE, kindly supplied by the *Southern Daily Echo,* shows the Southampton team which defeated Manchester United 1–0 in the 1976 FA Cup Final.
Back row (l to r) Jim Clunie, Pat Earls, Nick Holmes, Jim Steele, Peter Osgood, Ian Turner, Hugh Fisher, Mel Blyth, Paul Bennett.
Front row: Mick Channon, Paul Gilchrist, Jim McCalliog, Lawrie McMenemy (manager), Peter Rodrigues, Bobby Stokes, David Peach.

ABOUT THE AUTHOR

DEAN HAYES is an experienced freelance sports writer specialising in football and cricket.
He was educated at Hayward Grammar School, Bolton and West Midlands College of Physical Education. He was a primary school head teacher until taking up writing full-time three years ago.
Having played football in the Lancashire Amateur League, he now concentrates solely on playing the summer sport. This former cricket professional, now playing as an amateur, recently took his 2,000th wicket in league cricket.